VOICES OF AMERICA

LANCASTER COUNTY AND THE GREAT WAR

SOUTH CAROLINA

VOICES OF AMERICA

LANCASTER COUNTY AND THE GREAT WAR
SOUTH CAROLINA

Compiled by
John Chandler Griffin, Ph.D.

ARCADIA
PUBLISHING

ISBN 978-0-7385-0292-8

Published by Arcadia Publishing
Charleston, South Carolina

Printed in the United States of America

Library of Congress Catalog Card Number applied for.

For all general information contact Arcadia Publishing at:
Telephone 843-853-2070
Fax 843-853-0044
E-Mail edit@arcadiaimages.com

For customer service and orders:
Toll-Free 1-888-313-BOOK

Visit us on the Internet at www.arcadiaimages.com

Contents

The Kaiser, William II. (Note: In 1914, oddly enough, the kings of Germany, England, and Russia were first cousins, the grandsons of Queen Victoria.)

AUTHOR'S NOTE

In the process of compiling material for this historic look at Lancaster County's role in World War I, and do it in time to celebrate our nation's bicentennial (1976), it was our pleasure to interview more than 30 of our veterans of that terrible war.* There were others, of course, survivors of the Great War, whom we could not reach for one reason or another, and probably some whom we carelessly overlooked. To those we offer our sincere apologies. To all, we offer our respect, gratitude, and admiration.

We would also like to express our gratitude to both Charles Bundy of the Springs Foundation and Dianne Bailey of the Veterans Administration for recognizing the worth of the foregoing project and helping to make it possible.

Finally, we would like to offer a very special thanks to all those fine young students at USC-Lancaster who gave so cheerfully of their time and efforts to interview these veterans of the Great War. They did much of the work, and they deserve much of the credit. Listed in alphabetical order, they are:

Clarice F. Barnes
Amanda Bethea
Sarah Brenda Brown
Kathryn Buttermark
Deborah L. Calhoun
Betty R. Carnes
Charles H. Carr
Shuler Martha Connor
Janice Ingram
Jean Iseley
Melanie Hendricks
Martha G. Jackson
Vermell Lighter
Clyde T. Morgan
Ira Reeves
Kathy Scott

President Woodrow Wilson.

Blake Shute
William R. Steele
Carl D. Twitty
Rebecca Vassey
June C. Wade

*Note: These interviews were originally conducted in 1976. Today, in 1999, we would like to thank all those citizens of Lancaster County, the children and grandchildren of our Great War veterans, who came forward with their treasured photographs and other mementoes which the reader will find herein. This work would not have been possible without them.

Leaving Home

For almost three years the United States refused to be drawn into the deadly struggle that had tortured Europe since August 1914. Then, in April 1917, following the torpedoing of a great many American and Allied passenger ships, a clear violation of American neutrality, President Woodrow Wilson went before Congress and called for a declaration of war against Germany and its allies. Congress reacted immediately, and suddenly our nation entered what is today remembered as one of the most horrendous conflicts in the annals of warfare: The Great War of 1914-18.

THE LANCASTER NEWS

VOL. 12, No. 39. Semi-Weekly · Lancaster, S. C., Tuesday, April 3, 1917 · $1.50 A YEAR

PRESIDENT ASKED WAR DECLARATION

RESOLUTION INTRODUCED FOR BOTH SENATE AND HOUSE

Army of One-Half Million Men Asked For--- Champ Clark Is Again Chosen Speaker of House.

WAR RESOLUTION.

Washington, April 2.—Because of opposition to the war resolution of Senator Stone, chairman of the Foreign Relations Committee, the resolution was introduced in the Senate by Senator Martin, of Virginia, the Democratic floor leader, Representative Flood, chairman of the Foreign Affairs Committee, introduced it in the House. The resolution follows:

"Joint resolution declaring that a state of war exists between the Imperial German Government and the Government and people of the United States, and making a provision to prosecute the war:

"Whereas, The recent acts of the Imperial Government are acts of war against the Government and people of the United States;

"Resolved, By the Senate and House of Representatives of the United States of America in Congress assembled, that the state of war between the United States and the Imperial German Government, which has thus been thrust upon the United States, is hereby formally declared; and.

"That the President be and he is hereby, authorized and directed to take immediate steps not only to put the country in a thorough state of defense, but also to exert all of its power and employ all of its resources to carry on war against the Imperial German Government and to bring the conflict to a successful termination."

Washington, April 2.—President Wilson tonight asked Congress, assembled in joint session, to declare a state of war existing between the United States and Germany.

In a dispassionate but unmeasured denunciation of the course of the Imperial German Government, which he ... and autocratic power." Without selfish ends, for conquest or dominion, seeking no indemnities or material compensations for the sacrifices it shall make, the United States must enter the war, the President said, to make the world safe for democracy, as only one of the champions of the ...

GERMANY GATHERING ALL AVAILABLE MEN

CALLING ALL TO THEIR COLORS.

Von Hindenberg Hopes to See Great Campaign Bring War to Close This Year.

Copenhagen, April 1 (via London.)—Germany, according to information reaching here from Berlin, now is gathering to the colors every available man for a supreme military effort to bring the war to a victorious conclusion in this year's campaign—a goal which Field Marshal von Hindenburg and his advisers consider by no means impossible of attainment.

Without altering formally the law of military service the German authorities have in practice extended the period of service beyond the 45th year and are retaining with the colors and in many instances for fighting duty with active units in the front line, landstrum men who have passed this age. The policy of the German war department, as stated in the reichstag this week by a military representative, is to withdraw those men over 45 from the front line after they have done six months of duty there, but military exigencies compel the holding of these over-age men in reserve behind the actual fighting front.

For some time the German authorities have been mustering men on the very verge of the age limit but up to the present they announced that the necessity has not yet arisen for legislation raising the age limit to 65 as has been done in Austro-Hungary.

The operations of the labor service law, now in full swing, are further releasing for service at the front every available man behind the lines capable of carrying a rifle so that the next two or three months should see the German armies at their max-...

FORCE OF BRITISH NEARING ST. QUENTIN

CREEPING UP ON GERMAN STRONGHOLD.

English Thrust Line Trough Village and Wood on the Western Front.

The British forces in France are gradually creeping up on the important town of St. Quentin, considered one of the German strongholds. Also to the northwest of the town they are swinging their line forward at various points in a straightening out movement that is making good strides eastward.

Meanwhile the French forces under Gen. Nivelle are keeping up their offensive to the south and southeast of St. Quentin and again have made good progress north and south of Ailette river. They have captured several German trench systems and organized points of support east of Neuville Sur Margival inflicting heavy casualties on the Germans and driving them back to the outskirts of Vauxaillon and Laffaux.

West of St. Quentin the British have thrust their line through the village of Savy and the wood of Savy and now are resting only three miles from St. Quentin. Near Savy the Germans resisted tenaciously, but finally were beaten off, losing heavily in killed and wounded. To the north of this region the villages of ... on the St. Quentin ... road and ... have been taken by Field Marshal Haig's forces.

... suffered heavy losses.

The Lancaster News *of April 3, 1917 (Easter) announces that America is going to war.*

The people of Lancaster County were more than willing to meet the challenge. To answer our nation's call came men from all walks of life: textile workers, doctors, students, clergymen, postal workers, and even a watch maker. Still, in 1917, we were primarily a rural people, and "our boys" for the most part were young farm lads who had rarely, if ever, imagined that one day soon they would see the likes of New York, London, or Paris.

But they did, and most of them were glad for the experience. And most of them were just as glad to see Lancaster County again when it was all over.

The veterans we interviewed are in accord on one particular issue: to a man, they felt that our cause was just, and they were more than willing to do their bit. Typical is Bill Medford (30th "Old Hickory" Infantry Division) who says: "I was really patriotic about it. I thought our nation was right, and if they're in a war, I'll go with 'em. I wasn't just willing, I was downright eager to go. I just felt like if this country's worth living in, it's worth fighting for. And I still have that feeling today. I haven't changed a dern bit since then."

And former U.S. Senator J.P. Richards (30th "Old Hickory" Division) adds: "You see, we had the old fashioned idea back in those days that if you loved

JOIN THE
ARMY AIR SERVICE
BE AN AMERICAN EAGLE
CONSULT YOUR LOCAL DRAFT BOARD. READ THE ILLUSTRATED
BOOKLET AT ANY RECRUITING OFFICE, OR WRITE TO THE CHIEF
SIGNAL OFFICER OF THE ARMY, WASHINGTON, D.C.

NAMES OF DRAFTED MEN.

G. Otis Mobley.	Roddey Bell.
Robert L. Blackmon.	John W. Wright.
Willie Knight.	Clarence C. Crimminger.
Stanley Williams.	E. C. Bridges.
Will S. Adams.	Augustus Wright.
Ethell Maree.	Claude M. Steele.
George W. Culledge.	Lonnie S. Langley.
Julian H. Harris.	Joseph S. Hunter.
A Hoyt Bailey.	James J. Horton.
William L. White.	William C. Perry.
Robert L. Sistare.	William C. Wallace.
John E. Steele.	John N. Whitaker.
Will M. Benett.	William Spence.
Isaac Thomas.	Algie Vick.
Walter R. White.	Arthur Threatt.
Henry F. McManus.	C. E. Tiller.
Fred Harris.	Willis F. Ballard.
Edward C. Gooch.	William Sealey.
Edward H. Steele.	Ernest D. Barton.
Walter Threatt.	Lewis E. McManus.
John W. Massey.	Charley Knight.
Glenn P. Plyler.	Alvin R. Jones.
William J. Montgomery.	Ben Rollings.
John T. Bailey.	Carl T. Duren.
William B. Lemmond.	Henry E. Sowell.
James L. Ballard.	Lorain C. Ferguson.
Daniel C. Harris.	Judson L. Whitaker.
Ira L. Hinson.	Ben A. Garrison.
Jesse L. Hays.	Robert B. Culp.
John B. Faulkenberry.	Strait Parks.
David P. Roberts.	Ray V. Faile.
W. Connie Bowers.	Docton C. Outen.
Martin L. Stalling.	William E. Farmer.
J. R. Shehane.	Daniel C. Hinson.
Frank P. Bell.	Jack Garner.
Rodney Harris.	Cuthbert Gregory.
Ralph H. Hammond.	William C. Mehaffey.
	William C. Crimminger.

news from France became increasingly grim, with Allied soldiers being killed by the tens of thousands, Green decided to give it another try. To his satisfaction, the same doctor who had poked fun at him before gave him a quick look and said, "Green, the army took my nephew last week and he weighed only one-nineteen. So I don't think you're gonna get turned down. In fact, you're in."

Green says, "I never felt so grateful to one man before in my life." A year later he would be decorated for valor at the Battle of the Marne.

Nor were the heroic attitudes of our young recruits lost on the civilian population of Lancaster. There were parades down Main Street, speeches made in front of the Court House, and even receptions given in honor of those about to go to war.

Oscar Roddy Bell (30th "Old Hickory" Infantry Division) recalls: "The people of Lancaster gave us a big reception the night before we left. It was a very pleasant warm evening in late September 1917, and we all gathered in the armory space over the Bank of Lancaster. I was honored with a seat on the rostrum right between Leroy Springs and the Reverend Patterson, pastor of the A.R.P. Church. Then, the next morning eighty of us marched from the Court House down Main Street to the Southern Depot and boarded a train for Camp Jackson in Columbia. If only we'd known then what lay ahead!"

CAMP JACKSON

COLUMBIA, S. C.

will get a pass about the last of next week and come home to see youal, then I can tell you about my little girl I mean the one I go to see some times at Columbia she is so nice to me.

well I dont beleive I know any thing worth writing I just thought I would write you a few lines as I was writing to a few of my friends this morning Tell ma I said hello for me and be a good girl -

with lots of love to all John

Ben Tillman Wilson (right) of the Indian Land community was stationed with the 310th Quartermaster Corps at Fort Bliss, Texas. His friend, though unidentified, appears to have been something of a cowboy.

Camp Jackson in Columbia, South Carolina, is pictured above as it appeared in the fall of 1917. This postcard was sent home by Private Franklin Pierce Bell.

Ben C. Hough (Army Air Corps) remembers being assigned to Camp Sevier and reporting for early roll call on a bitterly cold morning in December 1917. He remembers standing there, teeth chattering, while his tough platoon sergeant kept tripping over the name H-o-u-g-h.

"Hove," shouted the sergeant.

No answer.

"Hue."

No answer. The irate sergeant glared at his platoon of young novices.

"Hoe," he bellowed.

No answer.

"HOG!"

At this point Hough reluctantly raised his hand and asked quietly, "Sir, is that Hough, H-o-u-g-h, that you're calling?"

The sergeant, his face red with anger, shook his fist and snarled at Hough, "Why you blanky-blank-blank, I'd kill my own brother for less than what you've done—keeping us out here in the snow like this."

"Well, I guess maybe he was right," laughs Hough, "but I made up my mind right then and there that if that man ever got in front of me when we got to France, I'd kill him. I meant it, and to this very day I don't entertain any nice feelings about him cursing me the way he did. I guess it's lucky for both of us that I never saw him once I left for France."

But for W.W. Stevenson (U.S. Navy) basic training was just a bit different. He underwent boot camp in Charleston, South Carolina, and recalls that when his Petty Officer called the roll he always did so in alphabetical order until he came to the last name on the roll—Stevenson. On one occasion, unfortunately, Stevenson was not paying attention, and that was the very time that the Petty Officer called the role in reverse.

"Stevenson, W. W."

No answer.

Twice more the Petty Officer bellowed, "Stevenson, W.W."

Still no response.

The exasperated Petty Officer then asked softly, "Would you gentlemen please remove your caps and read the name on the inside band?"

A barely audible "Here" came from Stevenson at that point. "I never felt so foolish in my life," grins Stevenson today. "And of course the other fellows got a big laugh out of it."

Following roll call the men would

Recruit John T. Bailey (top right) reported to Camp Jackson on September 19, 1917, for basic training. Within the next year, he would be in the thick of the fight in France.

Dickson Barnes Sistare was a young recruit at Camp Sevier in Greenville during the spring of 1918, when he was photographed here.

be marched to breakfast. There were hundreds to be fed at each chow hall, but only a few could be served at a time. Dr. Jesse Clyde Harris recalls that on his very first day in basic training he was put on K.P.

"I just couldn't seem to do anything right," he says, "so the sergeant saw to it that I was put where I couldn't do any harm." His job, he remembers, was to cook bacon for the entire company. After many slips and starts, he announced to the frustrated Mess Sergeant that he had it all down pat and that the bacon was finally "good and done." Unfortunately, by the time the bacon was ready, half the company, who had been standing at parade rest for the past hour under a broiling Camp Jackson sun, had passed out. Before the month ended Harris' company commander shook his hand and joked, "Harris, any man who can wipe out half a company in less than an hour must be a pretty good man." He then promoted Harris to sergeant.

As far as mess halls go, Grady Burgess had much better luck as a cook than did Dr. Harris. He remembers that he once cooked a delicious meal for his company commander, and from that time on he was considered a man of privileged position. Indeed, he will never forget the day his company was departing Camp Jackson for points of debarkation to France. He was standing in line to board a train along with some 200 other men when he looked up to see his platoon sergeant dashing towards him.

"And just what the hell are you doing here, Burgess?" he panted.

"Well, they say there's a war going on," Burgess cracked.

The distraught sergeant grabbed Burgess' speechless lieutenant by the arm. "The company commander says to get Burgess out of here. Says to replace him with George W. Bryan."

Charles S. Caskey (back row, right) is shown here with his senior classmates at the Douglas Community High School, c. 1910.

Recruits who were inducted in the summer of 1917 were dismayed to find that the army could equip them with neither rifles nor cannons, and thus they were forced to practice with pick handles and logs.

WORLD WAR

ROSTER

Company "F", 118th Infantry, United States Army, 59th Brigade, 30th Division

CAMP SEVIER, S. C.

First Lieutenant DAVID E. PENLAND *Commanding Company*

First Lieutenant JAMES A. SCHWING *First Lieutenat* WILLIAM W. JONES

Second Lieutenant TILLMAN H. SMITH

First Seargeant JAMES W. WOOD *Supply Sergeant* MILLS L. FLEMING *Mess Sergeant* WILLIAM H. KELLY

Company Clerk Corporal JAMES K. FINCH

SERGEANTS

JONES, BRONSON C.
FOSTER, GAREY E.
LANCE, PAUL G.
CHANDLER, THOMAS M.
LOVETT, OZZIE
FINE, CHARLES A.
ABERNATHY, THOMAS J.
GREEN, ALBERT L.
SHOOK, MARK M.
TROXELL, NORMAN

CORPORALS

MORGAN, EARNEST J.
CLINE, ROY C.
THOMAS, JOHN M.
STILL, JUTTIE S.
ATWELL, GROVER C.
BUTLER, LEVI H.
BECKHAM, WILLIAM T.
GOSSETT, WILLIAM L.
ALEXANDER, ERWIN
BIRD, JOHN P.
BOYD, JOHN J.
CROXDALE, CHARLES A.
COLE, JOHN G.
FINCH, JAMES K.
LEWIS, LAURIE B.
WEEKS, YOUMAN Z.
TUTTLE, DAVID C.
CROOKS, HENRY G.
DIAMOND, FRAMPTON L.
GREER, LINZIE B.
KIRBY, JOHN H.
STEWART, MARION R.
PARRIS, JACOB A.
SMITH, FARCE

MECHANICS

MORRIS, JOHN W.
OTT, WILLIAM D.
LANCE, FLOYD W.
HARVEY, SMITH J.

COOKS

GREEN, WILLIAM W.
KEARSE, JAMES C.
MORROW, TOM
WILLIAMS, HARRY P.

BUGLERS

GENTRY, HUGH E.
ABBOTT, ROYCE D.

PRIVATES, First Class

BAKER, CHARLIE
BEDENBOUGH, SAMMIE O.
BENTON, THOMAS E.
BLACK, LESLIE O.
BONDS, BENJIMIN T.
BROOM, WILLIAM D.
CADDADY, BIRL J.
COLLINS, JOHN R.
COKER, JOHN L.
COOK, EARNEST
COOPER, HAMPTON
CUDD, JOE C.
DEATON, LESTER S.
DUNN, LAND J.
FINE, WILLIAM M.
FLYNN, HENRY B.
GASTON, ROBERT L.
GREEN, OSCAR
HAM, DeWITT T.
HANNA, LEO
HARDEN, JAMES W.
HOWELL, PENCE H.
HOLT, TOM G.
HORTON, HAMPTON R.
HUNTER, CUSTER
JACKSON, ISAAC
JOHNSON, JAMES H.
KIRBY, ALONZO M.
LEMASTER, FERD
LITCHFIELD, HENRY T.
MAUPIN, GROVER C.
MEADOWS, BERNIE F.

PRIVATES, First Class

MORRIS, EDDIE
MOONEY, WILLIAM E.
NABERS, ALBERT N.
McFARLAND, OZZIE A.
McKINNEY, LOATER L.
PITTMAN, ALLIE G.
PULLUM, WILLIAM J.
PRICE, DOCTOR F.
RAWLES, EDDIE F.
REDMOND, WILLIAM H.
ROSE, GEORGE W.
SEALEY, WILLIAM G.
SEATON, JAMES
SMITH, LEROY W.
SMITH, HEBER B.
STEPHENS, WILLIAM J.
STOWE, CHARLIE D.
TREADWAY, HERSHEL
WADDY, FRANCIS R.
WASHAM, VIRGIL R.
WEIR, CLARENCE F.
WOOD, ALLEN
YOUMANS, ALBERT F., JR.

PRIVATES

ANDERSON, WILLIAM J.
ANDERSON, BERT L.
ADAMS, JADIE M.
BATES, ED A.
BRADLEY, ROE
BENNETT, WILLIAM M.
BLACKWELL, WILLIAM H.
BOGAN, TOMMIE
BOYKIN, JAMES W.
BOYKIN, JOHN I.
BRIGHT, WILLIAM T.
BUCKNER, FOREST B.
BURDEN, JONES
BUTLER, ROBERT C.
BYERS, GRESHAM
CANNON, ROY C.
CALDWELL, TOY T.

PRIVATES

CAMP, JACK F.
CAMPBELL, PAUL D.
CALDER, ARTHUR
CATHEY, BLUCHER
CHALK, RHADA L.
CHANDLER, ISAAC N.
CLAYTON, SIDNEY M.
CHRISTOFFERSON, H. T.
CLELLAND, CHARLES E.
COTHRAN, ALEX
COOPER, EARL R.
COOPER, FERRIS G.
DICKSON, JOHN L.
DILLARD, DOCTOR
DRIGGERS, JOHN M.
DRIVER, JOHN J.
DRUMMOND, WILLIAM E.
DRAKE, WILLIAM F.
FLEMING, McKINLEY
FLOYD, JAMES H.
FORSYTHE, GROVER C.
FOSTER, NORMAN
FOWLER, BOYCE L.
FOWLER, CHARLIE
FUELLING, W. A.
FUELLING, E. J.
GALLMAN, ROBERT
GEORGE, ALBERT
GOSSETT, ALBERT F.
GOWAN, IRA
GORDON, CLARENCE B.
GULDEN, IRA E.
HARLEY, JAMES M.
HARTL, FRANK J.
HAYNES, NORMAN N.
HARTLEY, CHARLIE
HARTER, EDWARD W.
HAYNIE, ALVIN
HARLEY, ONNIE W.
HARLEY, HERBERT L.
HARLEY, HENRY

PRIVATES

HAUGHEN, IRVIN
HAULBROOKS, JESSIE
HEGLAND, BERNHARD
HENDRICKS, JOHN C.
HICKINS, OLIVER E.
HOEL, LYNN F.
HOLCOMBE, JESSIE
JACKSON, JOE H.
JENSEN, EDGAR
JONES, CHALMERS H.
JONES, GEORGE F.
KEELING, JOHN
KIRBY, CLYDE T.
KITTELSON, WICHELY C.
KIESEL, LOUIS N.
KRUSE, FRED H.
KESKE, JOHN F.
LINDSEY, CRAWFORD
MANLEY, AARON B.
MATHIS, JAMES L.
MILLER, AARON B.
MILLWOOD, GROVER C.
MITCHELL, TOWNSDEN D.
MOZINGO, JAMES M. B.
MOORER, FRANK
MURPHY, J. F.
McABEE, WILLIAM
McCLELLAND, CLAY J.
McDOWELL, EDGAR
NEESE, CHARLIE E.
NODINE, NEVADA
OWENS, BENJIMIN T.
OWENS, JOSIAH C.
PARKER, JOE E.
PATRICK, NOYSE
PENLAND, IRA
PHILLIPS, RUFUS R.
POLLARD, JOE H.
PORCH, CHARLIE L.
PLATT, CHRISTOPHER C.
QUEEN, JOSEPH P.

PRIVATES

RAMSEY, WILL
REAVES, CLAUDE E.
RIEKNA, DICK N.
ROBERTSON, THOMAS W.
SANDLIN, CLARENCE B.
SANDERS, FRAMPTON L.
SAVAGE, ARCHIE
SAMMONS, JAMES L.
SANDERS, LEWIS M.
SANFORD, WILLIAM F.
SARRELS, JOHN H.
SEATON, BENJIMIN S.
SCHEWE, OTTO H.
SHARPE, PRESTON R.
SLICE, BEAUTRICE C.
SLITER, CHARLES A.
SMITH, JODIE P.
SMALL, OSCAR
STILL, AIKEN
STEWART, JAMES A.
STARK, ROBERT D.
TEAL, STEPHENS W.
THOMAS, C. A.
TURNEY, LEE ROY
TURNER, PINK
VARNADORE, MARTIN
VAUGHN, EDDIE M.
VICK, HEROLD I.
VIEROW, CARL H.
VIZENOR, I. D.
VOLTZ, HERMAN F.
WARDEN, JESSIE
WATERS, LEO
WATERS, CLARENCE E.
WENNDT, PAUL
WEST, PAUL J.
WESTMORELAND, E. B.
WILKE, EDWIN
WOLD, HARRISON
ZELLNER, HENRY G.

The roster of the 118th Infantry Regiment, 30th Infantry Division, was issued to Lancaster County's Pvt. William M. Bennett.

Remembering that event today, Burgess sadly shakes his head. "Six months later George Bryan was killed at Ypres. It should have been me."

But speaking of army food, still a favorite topic after all these years, Bill Medford says that many of the men found it strangely edible, while others found it merely strange. "But in all honesty, the food wasn't that bad. We'd have scrambled eggs, bacon, toast, coffee and orange juice for breakfast. I never found any reason to complain about it. It was better than what most of the fellows were getting back home."

Dr. L.W. Fort, on the other hand, says army food left something to be desired. Being a country boy, he especially missed turnip greens.

"I hadn't had any vegetables since kingdom come, looked like to me. Then one day I was sitting at this long table in the chow hall and I saw what looked like a bowl of turnip greens coming down. Well, I couldn't wait. I was really gonna fill up on those turnip greens. So I got me a big plate full and tasted them and my mouth sort of turned inside out. I turned to the fellow sitting next to me and I says, 'Say, boy, what in hell did they do to these turnip greens?' He says, 'Hell, these ain't turnip greens. I don't know nothing about turnips. This here's spinach.' I says, 'Well, this is the first damned time I ever tasted spinach. It won't make you sick?' Well, I ate it anyway. I didn't like it much, but I ate it. Well, about a week later I looked up and saw this okra coming down the table. By this time the boys were saying, 'What the hell's this slicky stuff? I can't keep it down.' I says, 'That's all right, boys, you caught me on the spinach. That's okra. I can eat it every day. It might take me two days, but I can eat every bit on this table.' And I almost did." (Dr. Fort, by the way, was already a dentist when inducted, and was commissioned a second lieutenant upon his completion of basic training.)

Joe Gandy stands here as a young recruit stationed at Chickamauga Park, Georgia. He soon fell victim to the flu and spent weeks in the base hospital. Still, despite the fact that he received no training, he was ordered to accompany his division to France.

Following breakfast the men of Lancaster County prepared themselves for a full day of training. Coyt Green recalls Camp Jackson and marching three miles to the rifle range every morning. "We'd never seen an army truck at that time. And we'd march three miles under that scorching sun, through that deep white sand, sweating, moaning, and complaining every morning. Then, when we got there, they'd hand us a pick handle to

William G. Jordan was inducted in May of 1918, took basic training at Camp Jackson, and was then assigned to Battery C, 316th Field Artillery until his discharge in June of 1919.

When Lancy Hilton completed basic training at Camp Jackson, his company was sent to Hoboken, New Jersey, where he and his company boarded a ship bound for France. Unfortunately, everyone aboard ship came down with mumps, the ship was quarentined, and the Armistice was declared before they could get into the Great War.

train with. Then we'd lie there going 'bang, bang!' There just weren't enough Springfield rifles to go around."

Howard K. Williamson (81st "Wildcat" Division) recalls, "As for our officers, most were from the South and treated the men with courtesy. But there was one officer at camp, a fellow from Pittsburgh, who tried to be hard. Later, in France he melted like butter when the Germans started shooting. He'd just lie in the bottom of the trench shaking and crying. And he couldn't find a friend anywhere to help him out."

Vance Bailey agrees that most officers were pretty decent fellows. "I got along real well with our officers, and our sarge was a pretty good guy too. I remember one day we had a field review parade, and they had us out there marching with the other companies. I think the President or somebody important was there. Well, we marched by and then they had us march by again. I just couldn't figure that out for a while. Come to find out though, we were selected the best drilled company in camp, so that shows you we had a good group of officers. It was hot as the devil down there and our officers would march us in the shade when it got too hot, so you can see they were okay."

James H. Caskey (76th Infantry Division) assumed that basic training would be a cakewalk for him, since he'd farmed all his life and "was used to the hot sun and hard work." But he, like 90 percent of his company, "collapsed during our first 20-mile hike."

By the time evening rolled around the men were deeply fatigued and were more than ready for a little rest and relaxation. Dr. J.C. Harris remembers that they were paid only $15 a month and there was no place to spend that. So the men made up their own diversions. "They especially liked to sit around and sing," says Dr. Harris.

Henry Hazel Starnes (fourth from left) can be seen with his Coastal Artillery Battery. Following basic training, he was stationed at Camp Pensacola in Florida.

Camp Pensacola actually didn't exist when Starnes and his company arrived there. Thus, they were set to work building barracks, sidewalks, and roads.

Charles Caskey (standing, left) and Ira L. Pittman (seated) posed while on duty in New Jersey. Both were with the 302nd Fire and Guard.

Seaman Yancy W. Hinson while stationed at the Charleston Navy Yard. Assisgned to the Provost Guard, he was on duty when this photograph was taken in 1918.

"Songs helped pass the time, as well as drown out the lonely feelings many of us had during those first weeks of basic training. And of course there was always some fellow handy who could play a guitar, so we'd have some pretty good songfests. Some of our favorites were *Sweet Adeline, Round the Street, A Long Way to Tipparari* and *Long Boy,* which goes like this:"

Great big long lean country gink,
From way out west where the hoppy toads wink;
Six foot two in stocking feet,
Keeps getting thinner the more he eats.

At Camp Gordon, Georgia, where Dr. Harris later attended Officers Candidate School, the favorite song of all the soldiers was *Gonna Ride That Gold Bar Special One Of These Days—Hallelujah.* This song concerns a special train with a gold bar painted on the side that the men could ride into Columbus—if they were fortunate enough to complete OCS.

Later, after the men reached France, their favorite songs, according to Leonard Thurlow Hallman (21st Heavy Artillery, 5th Division), were *It's You I'm Fighting For* and a humorous ditty entitled *I Want A Piece of Your Rhine.*

"Oh, we'd sing that sad song—*Goodbye sweethearts, wives and mothers. It won't take us long. It's you we're fighting for*—that was pretty and sad too," says Hallman. "Mothers couldn't stand to hear that song. They'd cry every time." Hallman grins good naturedly. "As for the Rhine song, it goes: *I don't want your bacon, I don't want your bacon. All I want is a piece of your Rhine."*

Basic training proved a valuable experience to many, one that prepared them well to meet the rigors of France. But for others it proved a study in frustration. For Ben C. Hough, a watch maker prior to the war, it seemed a waste of time.

"All day we trained. We marched around, we marched this way and that way and stood on our heads, just did all sorts of different maneuvers and obeyed all sorts of different commands. Yet when I arrived in France they assigned me to an aviation depot and I spent the whole war repairing airplane instruments. I didn't march a step or see a rifle the whole time I was there." Hough smiles and shakes his head. "Well, I guess I did spend some time down in the trenches, but most of my time was spent repairing instruments."

W.B. Adams says the thing he hated most about basic training was taking shots. "I remember standing in those long lines and taking those typhoid shots. There was a fellow standing on each side of you, and when you walked up they'd go bing-bing, a shot in each arm. Well, the first two I took didn't bother me, but the third one almost killed me. By that evening my tongue got thick and dry. I went back to our tent and lay in my bunk and drank water all night that a buddy would bring me. The next morning my lips were swollen huge like two big slabs of fatback, and I was so sick I couldn't get out of bed. I couldn't have answered reveille even if they'd threatened to shoot me."

In a word, according to L.O. McManus (21st Field Artillery, 5th Division), basic training was hardly a paradise. "Do you want it plain? It was hell. Just like hell. All of it. You've read about hell in the Bible, haven't you? Well, that's the way it was. Just like hell."

And that, it would seem, about says it all.

Yet to a man, the men of Lancaster County were eager to do their bit. Typical is Willie B. Hoke (82nd "All American" Infantry Division), who landed in France as a combat engineer at the ripe old age of 16.

"I wasn't blood thirsty, but I was determined to fight for America. My

Will T. Hair (Company E, 2nd Provisional Regiment, Camp Sevier) stands by Henry Mattox (Company H, 7th Provincial Line Regiment, Camp Jackson).

William W. Stevenson, born in Richburg, met famed artist Norman Rockwell while in training at the Charleston Naval Yard in July of 1918. He later served aboard the U.S.S. Vixen.

This postcard is from Sim Plyler, who is pictured on page 83.

Banquet Was Given to 76 Men Who Left in September 1917 For Camp Jackson.

The following story appeared in the issue of Friday, Sept. 21, 1917, under the heading "Lancaster Tells Soldier Boys Goodbye."

On Wednesday night, Sept. 19 a patriotic banquet was given the seventy-six men of the national army representing Lancaster's second quota under the "selected draft act" and who left on Thursday morning for Camp Andrew Jackson where they will be trained.

The drafted boys met at the court house at 7 o'clock where they formed a line and marched down to the Mackey Opera House where this banquet was held. The opera house was beautifully decorated for the occasion by the ladies of the Red Cross. The banquet was arranged and financed by the citizens of the town of Lancaster by contributions to give the boys a cheerful send-off.

After supper was rendered by the Lancaster orchestra which consisted of Mr. and Mrs. John Poag, Maney and Ben Hirsch, R. Thomas Beaty and Mr. McDermid. Then the smoker and speeches began with talks by Rev. W. S. Patterson, Rev. Hugh R. Murchison, Judge Ira B. Jones, R. S. Stewart, Roddey Bell and W. G. A. Porter.

Thursday morning at 8:30 o'clock the boys all met at the court house and were escorted to the depot by the Boy Scouts to the tune of fife and drum under the leadership of Scoutmaster John H. Poag. A large gathering of friends and relatives of those young men were at the depot to witness their departure and bid them goodbye.

The following are the names of the boys who left for Columbia:

G. Otis Mobley, Robert L. Blackmon, Willie Knight, Stanley Williams, Will S. Adams, Ethel Maree, George W. Gulledge, Julian H. Harris, A. Hoyt Bailey, William L. White, Robert L. Sistare, John E. Steele, Will M. Bennett, Isaac Thomas, Walter R. White, Henry F. McManus, Fred Harris, Edward C. Gooch, Edward H. Steele, Walter Threatt, John W. Massey, Glenn P. Plyler, William J. Montgomery, John T. Bailey, William B. Lemmond, James L. Ballard, Daniel C. Harris, Ira L. Hinson, Jesse L. Hays, John R. Faulkenberry, David P. Roberts, W. Connie Bowers, Martin L. Stalling, J. R. Shehane, Frank P. Bell, Roddey Harris, Ralph H. Hammond, Roddey Bell, John W. Wright, Clarence C. Crimminger, E. C. Bridges, Augustus Wright, Claude M. Steele, Lonnie S. Langley, Joseph S. Hunter, James J. Horton, William C. Perry, William C. Wallace, John N. Whitaker, William Spence, Algie Vick, Arthur Threatt, C. E. Tiller, Willies F. Ballard, William Sealey, Ernest D. Barton, Lewis E. McManus, Charley Knight, Alvin R. Jones, Ben Rollins, Carl T. Duren, Henry E. Sowell, Lorain C. Ferguson, Judson L. Whitaker, Ben A. Garrison, Robert B. Culp, Strait Parks, Ray V. Faile, Docton C. Outen, William E. Farmer, Daniel C. Hinson, Jack Garner, Cuthbert Gregory, William C. Mahaffey, William C. Crimminger.

brothers were in France, and I was determined to go too. At first they wouldn't take me because of my age, and I was getting ready to go to Canada and enlist. But then the American army agreed to take me. I was only 16, you see." (Hoke might well have been the youngest of our veterans to see combat in France.)

As for Dr. J.C. Harris, he would do anything for America, he says, take on any job, but when his captain ordered him to become the company bugler, he drew the line.

"No, Sir," he said. "You can just give me my discharge."

His captain glared at him in disbelief. "What's the matter with you, Harris? Are you crazy?"

"No, Sir," Harris replied, "but if you can't offer me anything better than a job standing under a tree tooting a damned horn all day, you can just let me go home."

Within a short while Harris was promoted to sergeant and then sent to Officers Candidate School. In time he would become well known for his expertise in instructing recruits, a great many of whom were from Lancaster and assigned to the famous 81st "Wildcat" Division.

Lee Skipper had been fascinated by flying and aeroplanes for as long as he could remember, or at least since the Wright brothers had flown their first glider at Kitty Hawk in 1906. Thus once America declared war on Germany he took a train to Washington, D.C., and visited the army's Air Service

At home on leave for Easter of 1918, Henry Hazel Starnes is here surrounded by his proud parents and four brothers.

Henry Starnes' battery overlooked the Gulf of Mexico and protected the entrance to Pensacola.

Headquarters. There he passed tests which proved that he had the intelligence to master the intricacies of flying. Then he was sent to the Georgia Tech Ground School (Signal Officers Reserve Corps.). On November 3, 1917, he completed his pilot's training, and he had the gold bar of a second lieutenant penned on his shoulders and his silver pilot's wings penned on his chest. A month later, he says, he was engaged in aerial combat against the Germans over France.

The highlight of W.W. Stevenson's boot camp training career was the day he met famed artist Norman Rockwell down at the Charleston Naval Station.

"It was a hot Sunday in the summer of 1917, with the sun crashing down the way it does in Charleston, and they had me running messages at headquarters. I remember this young lieutenant came out and told me to go down to the Knights of Columbus hut, a building run by Catholics, and see if I could find Norman Rockwell. Well, it was hot, I mean really hot, and the sand came up to my knees, and I ran for about a mile until I reached the KC hut. But then, once I walked in the door, I suddenly couldn't remember who I'd been sent to find.

"So I ran back through the heat and the sand to headquarters, but I didn't tell them I couldn't remember the soldier's name I'd been sent to find. So this same lieutenant came out again and said, 'Did you find Rockwell?' I said, 'Nobody down there's seen him.' So he said, 'Well, you go back down there and stay till he comes. He'll be there. He's Catholic and all the Catholics'll be there.' So this time I wrote the name down. Then I ran back to the KC hut and told the officer at the door who I was looking for. So he went inside and a few minutes later Rockwell came out. I said, 'They want you down at headquarters.' He looked sort of scared

and he asked, 'Whatta they want me for?' And I said I didn't know. Well, we started back and it was still hot and the sand still came up to my knees, and Rockwell kept saying, 'Whatta they want with me? What've I done?' Well, the thing was, as it turned out, they'd found out he could draw and they wanted him to draw some things for this little old paper they were putting out. Rockwell was a little dried up fellow but pleasant enough."

In 1917, according to Oscar Roddy Bell, a division was composed of two brigades; a brigade of 2 regiments; and a regiment of 15 companies. Among the various Divisions served by Lancaster's veterans, the following received prominant mention: the 2nd, 5th, 6th, 27th, 30th, 37th, 76th, 81st, 82nd, and the 97th. Most of our men received their division assignments upon completion of basic training.

Henry R. Mattox (156th Depot Brigade, 2nd Infantry Division) was almost killed in basic training when he was pinned beneath an overturned truck for some 90 minutes. After five weeks in an army hospital, he was told that his arm would

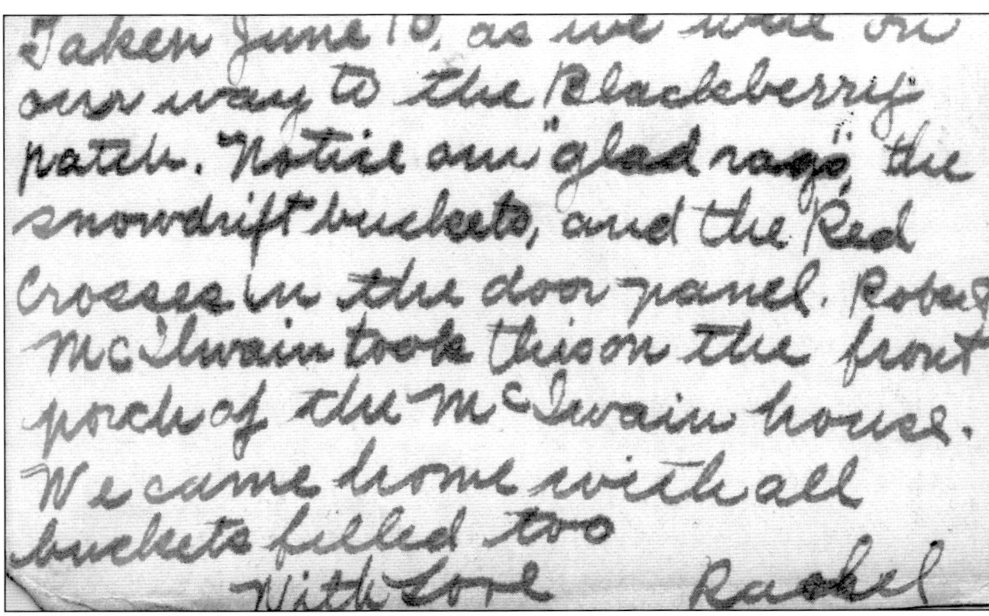
Taken June 10, as we were on our way to the Blackberry patch. Notice our "glad rags," the snowdrift buckets, and the Red Crosses in the door panel. Robert McIlwain took this on the front porch of the McIlwain house. We came home with all buckets filled too
With Love Rachel

SOLDIERS' MAIL.

THE AMERICAN RED CROSS

MILITARY POST OFFICE SOLDIERS MAIL

NO POSTAGE NECESSARY.

THIS SIDE FOR ADDRESS ONLY.

Mrs G L Mobley
Heath Springs
U.S.A. South Carolina

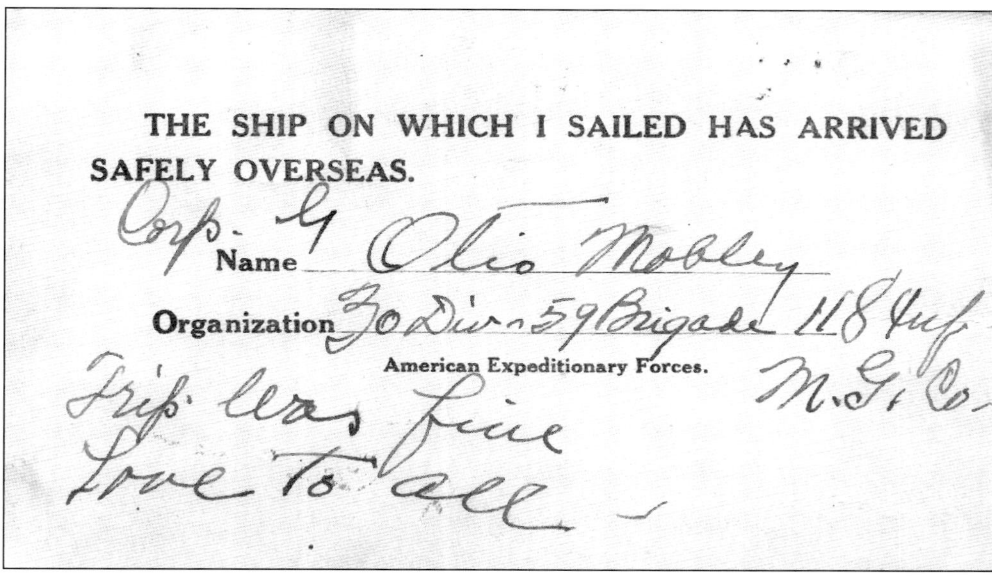

THE SHIP ON WHICH I SAILED HAS ARRIVED SAFELY OVERSEAS.

Name Corp. G Olio Mobley

Organization 30 Div. 59 Brigade 118 Inf. M.G. Co.

American Expeditionary Forces.

Trip was fine
Love to all

have to be amputated. "But I told them I had faith enough to believe I could find a man who could cure my arm. So I just walked out on them. I came back to Lancaster then, and went to see Dr. Carl Lippard and be darned if he didn't cure me."

Jim Cauthen fell ill with the flu during basic training. Back in those days, he recalls, the flu was considered a deadly disease. "You either died, or you spent months in bed." The latter fate befell Cauthen, and he was transferred from Camp Jackson to a hospital in Greenville, where he spent the remainder of the war.

Joe Gandy was not as fortunate as Jim Cauthen. Stationed at Chickamauga Park, Georgia, for basic training, he too fell ill with the flu, and only two days after he arrived there. For three weeks he lay in the hospital, hovering between

Fred Horton was an eager recruit at Fort Screven, Georgia, in 1917. He has written on this photo which he sent to his parents: "Ready to Go" and "Show the Kaiser to me."

life and death. Then one freezing cold morning in February of 1918 an orderly roused him out of bed and told him that his regiment was leaving immediately for France and that he was going with them. Gandy was flabbergasted, since at this point he had no knowledge of army life whatsoever, except what little he had been able to glean from his hospital bed. But that did not stop the army. And sure enough, he was handed his equipment and boarded a train for New York. Upon his arrival, he immediately boarded a troop ship and was sent straight to France. There, since his only military experience was gained in an army hospital, he was assigned to work as a medic in Base Hospital Number-78, a job he would hold until the Armistice was signed in November 1918.

And We Won't Be Back Till It's Over, Over There

Unlike the great majority of our veterans, who were sent first to England and then to France following basic training, Dr. L.W. Fort, by now a second lieutenant, found himself stationed at Camp Wadsworth in Spartanburg, only 100 miles from home. (He would soon receive permanent assignment to Ft. McHenry in Maryland.) A lifelong farm boy, Fort knew a great deal about horses and was initially assigned the task of overseeing the training of mules.

Dr. L.W. Fort (seen here with his arm around a friend's shoulders) entered the army as a private, but after three weeks was promoted to second lieutenant. At Camp Wadsworth, he was assigned to the 54th Pioneer Infantry, but then was sent on to Ft. McHenry in Maryland.

"The army hauled wood all the way from Kings Mountain to Spartanburg. Dumbest thing I ever saw. They could have gotten wood right there. And those Northern fellows didn't know a bit how to handle mules. They had the wheel mules up front and the lead mules in back, the opposite of where they should have been. Well, the mules had enough sense to know they had 'em backwards, but those Yankees didn't. I said, 'Wait a minute, fellows, let me see.' I got up there and I pulled the lead mules in front, and the wheel mules in back and didn't let go until I had 'em all going. One of the Yankees said, 'By God, he knows how to talk to mules, don't he?' I said, 'No, but I do know how to hitch 'em up.' "

Dr. Fort also remembers that the winter of 1917 was bitterly cold. He remembers his first night at Ft. Wadsworth and that he and his company were given tent pegs and told to erect shelters.

"Man," he laughs, "it was so cold and the ground was frozen so hard that you couldn't have put those pegs down with a jackhammer." But Fort had a solution. "They'd been erecting a batch of buildings and they had some lumber cut up in

Henry Mattox as he appeared at Camp Jackson in July 1918, just days following his medical discharge from the army.

Henry Mattox with his younger brother Walter pose in this photograph taken in 1916, the year before Mattox's induction. It should be noted that they are decked out in their Sunday finest for this shot, both wearing the knickers that were so popular with the young men of this era.

three-foot-long sections. And there was a new mess hall in a field over to our right. So I turned to the boys in my company and I told 'em, 'Get an arm load of wood, and let's all go in that empty mess hall over there and make a fire so we won't freeze to death. One of us will have to stay awake all night to keep it going, and that's all there is to it.' Well, those fellows were very grateful that I put 'em in there and told 'em to stay warm. We played cards by the fire light and amused ourselves the best way we could. And nobody ever knew the difference."

Francis L. Schwartz was trained as a Medical Corpman after basic training and sent to a large hospital at Ft. Oglethorpe, Georgia, where he would spend the entire war. He was terribly disappointed, he says, that he did not get to experience France and frontline warfare, but once casualties began arriving at the hospital, he saw that he could do more good at the hospital than in the trenches.

For Lee Montgomery (U.S. Navy) the completion of basic training in Charleston meant permanent assignment in Hampton Roads, Virginia. His most vivid memory of the war concerns a certain comrade—a huge coal miner from Pennsylvania called Guard Dog.

"We'd go on liberty, and if there was any trouble, Guard Dog would take my side. In other words, if someone said something to me I didn't like, I'd just growl, 'Guard Dog' and he'd give somebody a good punch in the nose. For two years I was the bravest man in Hampton Roads."

But Fort, Schwartz, and Montgomery were exceptions to the general rule. For most of our veterans, completion of basic training meant a long train ride to Camp Merritt, New Jersey, or to Long Island, New York, where they would await the great ships that would take them to France.

As the landscape of the eastern seaboard rolled by, with little to distract them, they whiled away the hours as best they could.

James H. Caskey (76th Infantry Division) says, "That train ride will always linger in my memory. For it was then that we sang some of the most popular songs of the day—*The Yanks Are Coming* and *Over There* among others. I really enjoyed the whole trip and got to see a lot of country I'd never seen before."

Bill Medford and his company whiled away the hours on their way to New York "doing most anything, nothing in particular. Often some very charming ladies would come down and meet the troop trains, wave at us and smile, you know. In some places, down in the Carolinas especially, some of the wives would try to see their husbands. Some of the men were married and had children, and they would get off the train and try to speak to their families. I recall once, right outside New Jersey, some of us jumped off to see some young ladies who were standing there by the side of the tracks, and the train pulled out and left us. But we knew where we were supposed to go, and we hired a taxi and it took us to camp. We were a little late, but we got in."

Once in New York, James H. Caskey, accompanied by his old Lancaster chum, Brice Montgomery, "had high hopes of obtaining an overnight pass and living it up a little. Unfortunately, or fortunately, I don't know which, we were immediately ordered aboard ship. Six hours later we departed for France. So that was the end of our big sightseeing trip around New York."

But Lady Luck was considerably more kind to Bill Medford. He remained in New York for several weeks, during which time he met many fine people and saw many interesting sights. He and a friend met "some very charming ladies

Henry Pitts was inducted in September 1918 and received basic training at Camp Jackson. He was a member of the 156th Depot Brigade until his discharge in March 1919.

Ira Harper, who stood well over six feet tall, dwarfs his two unidentified counterparts in this photograph taken in France in 1918.

This Bill Medford photograph shows a few of the 120,000 American troops being shipped to Europe monthly in the fall of 1917. These convoys were constantly tracked by German U-boats and dozens were sent to the bottom.

Bill Medford of the 30th Infantry Division (top right) was so bored with life aboard ship that he would have welcomed a torpedo attack. He would see heavy combat almost immediately upon his arrival in France (as would most others of the 30th Infantry).

up there. We went out to their homes with them. Soldiers were at a premium at that time, and they were real nice to us, very respectable girls. We would spend the evening at their homes, or go to a movie. I remember seeing *The Perils of Pauline* up there. Then we'd go back to their homes and sing while one of the girls played the piano. Sometimes we'd do a little courting on the side. We sang such songs as *Long, Long Trail A-Winding* and *K-K-K-Katie.* I think Kate Smith sang that back in those days. And also *Oh, How I Hate To Get Up In The Morning* and *Over There.*"

The experiences of Oscar Roddy Bell following basic training are typical of many. He departed Camp Sevier, South Carolina, for Camp Mills, New York, where he remained for ten days. Then he was taken by rail to Hoboken, New

Lt. Lee Skipper was a pilot for the Signal Corps of the Army Air Service. He flew reconnaissance as well as bombing missions for the Allies. Deadly dogfights over the trenches of France were a daily occurance and Skipper was lucky to survive the war.

remembers many confrontations with U-boats while ferrying troops across the Atlantic.

"I remember on one occasion we cornered a U-boat and dropped depth charges until the U-boat was forced to surface. We captured the U-boat commander and 15 members of his crew. And I'll tell you now, those German sailors were pretty nice chaps. And we certainly didn't subject them to harsh treatment. In fact, believe it or not, when we went on liberty in New York, we took them with us. They didn't have anywhere to go, so we just told 'em to clean up and we'd take in the sights. And we all had a great time. They certainly didn't try to escape or anything. In fact, they probably had it better aboard *The Wainwright* than aboard the U-boat."

For Bill Medford and many others, after weeks of humdrum shipboard life, the sighting of a U-boat, instead of striking terror into the hearts of all aboard, was a cause for jubilation. Indeed, he recalls that on one occasion, several days out from Nova Scotia, the alert was sounded and he excitedly ran up on deck to see what was going on.

"We all went up. Every one of us. We were all crowded on deck, hanging over the railing, and betting with one another that we would get torpedoed or that we wouldn't get torpedoed. Just a nice warm delightful afternoon on that beautiful blue Atlantic Ocean, and we were just a bunch of youngsters with no cares about us. Really, we just didn't realize how deeply we were involved or what a torpedo could do to us."

As though the U-boats were not enough to contend with, a number of our soldiers seem to have suffered from seasickness from the time they left America until they arrived in England or France.

Nearly All Well.

The six patients now at the mill hospital are recovering satisfactorily and will leave the hospital today or tomorrow. Unless new cases develop or old ones grow more serious, the epidemic will be passed in this city, though there are still numerous cases in the city and mill village cared for in the homes.

—o—

Off to Camp.

The following left this morning for Camp Wadsworth, Spartanburg:

Meridith Baker, Charley B. Baker, James L. Ballard, Thomas L. Ballard, Earl H. Belk, Walter E. Blackmon, Frank Blackwell, Ben F. Caldwell, Otis Dees, John F. Funderburk, Darling Harris, Thos. J. Holden, Robert Hazel Mosier, Frank Rice, Leroy Roberts, Benjamin F. Self, Hiram T. Steele, John C. Stogner, Thurman West.

—o—

Only Five Deaths Since Thursday.

The epidemic of influenza in this city and at the Lancaster cotton mills has passed the crest and is now being fast overcome. Only five deaths were recorded with the registrar of vital statistics for Lancaster and suburbs from Thursday morning until this morning, four being due to influenza and pneumonia. They were as follows:

Arthur Harper, colored, died October 30; pneumonia; age 23.

Clyburn Threatt, died November 1; influenza; age six; son of O. H. Threatt.

Thurlow Ingram, died November 3; influenza; age seven.

F. M. Sellers, died November 4; pneumonia; age 48.

Nanza Laney, colored, died November 2; age one.

—o—

Prices Are Mounting.

Prices of some commodities and confections and fruits particularly have mounted so that the average person of moderate means feels they are beyond the realms of his pocketbook, although he is admonished daily, if not oftener, to eat more fruits. There have been numerous complaints in this city recently of the prices charged for fruits and confections.

Apples are selling at fifty cents the dozen. They are reasonably good apples and sometimes very good.

Bananas sell at fifty cents the dozen.

Oranges at seventy-five cents the dozen.

Brazil nuts and English walnuts at fifty cents the pound.

—o—

Mrs. J. Reece Funderburk, who has been seriously ill with pneumonia at the home of W. P. Robinson, is much improved.

—o—

Mrs. H. N. Sowell and Mrs. R. A. Long returned Saturday from Rock Hill where they went for treatment at the Fennell infirmary. Both underwent serious operations, but are now fast improving.

—o—

F. R. Hay, who has been critically ill with pneumonia at his home on North Catawba street, is reported today as having spent a comparatively satisfactory night and his condition is thought to be better.

—o—

Mrs. W. A. Davis and Miss Bernice Davis spent the week-end in Charlotte with Mr. and Mrs. George Heath.

—o—

Irvin Jackson, who has been timekeeper for the Lancaster cotton mills for several years, left Saturday for Jeffersonville, Ind., where he has accepted a position as cloth inspector for the government.

ONE OF BEST FIGHTERS AMERICA HAS IN AIR

Prof. Paul Van Dyke, of Paris, Thus Writes of Lieutenant Elliott W. Springs.

Col. Leroy Springs has received the following letter, which will be of keen interest to his friends and those of his son, Elliott Springs:

American University Union in Europe, 8 Rue de Richelieu, Royal Palace Hotel.

Princeton Bureau, 16 Pall Mall, East S. W. I., Paris October 11, 1918.

My Dear Mr. Springs:

I just drop you a line to say that your son, Elliott, has been in to see us several times recently. He has a good long leave at Paris, which he has thoroughly earned. Perhaps he is too modest to tell you, but he is one of the very best fighters America has in the air and has already won a great many victories. He seems to be very well. I hope we shall see him frequently during his stay in Paris.

Believe me,

Yours very sincerely,

(Signed) Paul Van Dyke.

IN MEMORIAM.

throughout the entire county. To over the top every time in eve shipment as the Lancaster chapt has done, cannot be said of many o ganizations.

The money one invests in W. S. quickly becomes transformed to bullets that rid the world Huns.

CITATION FOR LETTERS OF A MINISTRATION.

STATE OF SOUTH CAROLINA
County of Lancaster.

By J. E. Stewman, Judge of P bate.

Whereas Mrs. Eula D. Cunni ham and W. J Cunningham h made suit to me to grant them l ters of Administration of the est and effects of R. Frank Cunni ham, deceased.

These are, therefore, to cite admonish all and singular the dred and creditors of the said ceased, that they be and appear fore me, in the Court of Probate be held at Lancaster on 20th N 1918, next, after publication ther at 11 o'clock in the forenoon, show cause, if any they have, the said Administration should be granted.

Given under my hand, this day of November Anno Domini 19

J. E. STEWMAN,
Probate Jud

BUSINESS NOTICES

THE LANCASTER NEWS TUESDAY, OCT. 23, 1917

ELLIOTT WHITE SPRINGS

An officer in the American avaiation corps, somewhere in Europe, Mr. Springs has not yet received his commission, but is soon to be lieutenant. He is a son of Col. Leroy Springs of Lancaster. His paternal ancestors, Col. A. Baxter Springs and Capt. Samuel Elliott White, were men of note in their day. Elliott Springs ... A. R. Banks, graduated from ... ver, the great military school in ... diana, in 1913, and was in the g... uating class at Princeton this y... He was among the honor men ... was in the uniform of a private ... dier of the United States when ... received his diploma. Along ... many other Princeton men he jo...

W.B. Adams says, "The first few days out to sea the weather was nice and the sea very calm. Then about a week out a violent storm came up and pitched our ship from side to side, just as though it was a little cork. That lasted nine days and nights. I became deathly ill. I remember lying on the deck vomiting when someone tapped me on the shoulder and said there was a U-boat off our bow and that we might get torpedoed. I held my head and moaned, 'The sooner the better.'"

Likewise feeling that he was at the point of death, Howard K. Williamson remembers "trying to force down a sausage and pickle between two slices of bread, but it was no use." Then he paid a friend 25 cents for a Hershey Bar, but it was money wasted. "You just lie in your hammock," says Williamson, "15 feet below water level, hot, cramped, sweating like the devil, with only 12 inches of space between hammocks. At first you're afraid you're gonna die. Then you're afraid you won't. I remember on one occasion the captain gave the order for everyone to hit the deck. I finally managed to rise up and get to my feet. There was a lieutenant from Pennsylvania and he got to the ladder just ahead of me, but that was as far as he got. 'Can I give you a hand?' I asked him. 'Just get out of the way,' he said, pushing me out of the way. And I did—fast!"

The primary cause of seasickness was doubtlessly the rough weather. But then the food didn't seem to help much either. Bill Medford recalls that there was just too much lamb meat.

"As you might expect from a bunch of 18 year old roughnecks, we called it goaty. And the more we chewed it, the more we had to chew it."

W.B. Adams recalls a joke that was making the rounds during his crossing of the Atlantic. "It seems there was this chaplain who got very nervous and upset because the sea was so rough. So he went up to the captain and asked if it was time to start praying. To this the captain replied, 'You see all those men shooting dice everywhere? Well, when they stop shooting dice, it's time to start praying.' So the chaplain then ran around the ship watching the soldiers shooting dice. Finally he ran back to the captain and said, 'Thank God! The men are still gambling.'"

Adams himself became quite seasick during the crossing. He remembers hanging over the railing, feeling that he was at the point of death when one of his friends patted him on the back and asked if he had a weak stomach. "Are you kidding?" Adams replied. "I'm throwing it just as far as any man on this ship."

Leonard Thurlow Hallman (21st Heavy Artillery, 5th Infantry Division) recalls that every man was required to write one letter home during the crossing.

The American aerodrome at Issoudum. It was here that Lt. Lee Skipper was stationed for most of the war.

Yet the men could mention neither conditions aboard ship nor anything else that pertained to the military. "In fact, there we were in the middle of the Atlantic, yet we were ordered to write that we had arrived safely in France and that all was well. Every man had to write that. I remember I sent my preacher a letter, and the next Sunday he announced in church that I had landed in France and that the war was all but over. At that point I'd never even seen an enemy soldier."

After two weeks of U-boats and seasickness on the high, gray seas of the North Atlantic, England must have seemed a true Promised Land to our veterans.

"It was springtime in England," remembers Oscar Roddy Bell, "and I've never seen a more wonderful country than the area from Liverpool down to Folkstone, which is just down the road from Dover on the Channel." He remembers his company marching out onto a long pier where a mounted British soldier was directing traffic. "That Britisher was dressed lavishly in a red coat and blue trousers with gold braid going everywhere. Somebody behind me remarked, 'Good God, it looks like they've sent the king of England himself down to meet us.'"

Many of the men remained in Folkstone, other were sent to Dover. As guests of the British, they were quartered in two story wooden barracks, where they found they'd been furnished neither bunks nor light bulbs. They were thus forced to make their way around in the darkness as well as they could, and to sleep on the floor.

It was here that many of the men, especially those of the 30th Division, now attached to the British 4th Army, traded their American equipment for British. They were given Enfield rifles, steel helmets, and odd looking brogans which would fit either foot.

Lt. Elliott White Springs, the fifth-ranking American air ace in World War I, was assigned to the 58th Squadron, Royal Air Force. He participated in both the Picardy and Somme offensives. He received both the American Distinguished Service Cross and the British Distinguished Flying Cross for bravery. He is shown here with his British Sopwith Camel fighter.

Many of these men say they developed a strange yearning for tea at four p.m. every afternoon.

Our veterans recall that they first set foot on French soil at such ports as Calais, Brest, and Bordeaux, all many miles from the front lines, and known as the "Blue Zone" or the "Quiet Zone."

Lee Skipper, who had completed his pilot's training at Georgia Tech, had been in France for several months when the first Lancaster soldiers began to arrive. He himself had made the

John H. Hinson (Battery E, 135th Field Artillery). "An artillery round has no conscience," he said, still recoiling in horror at the memory of those big shells landing indiscriminately among friend and foe alike, spreading death and destruction.

crossing from New York aboard *The Baltic,* and was then stationed briefly at Bordeaux. Then he underwent additional flight training at various French flight schools (Ecole d' Aviation) at Chartes, Avord, Tours, and Issoudun. These facilities, he says, were primitive, with the men sleeping in tents and barns, and training for combat in French planes that had obviously seen better days.

Yet, as compared with the miserable life of the infantry, life for the airman was luxurious. For example, Skipper remembers spending many evenings attending balls and champagne parties. While his infantry brothers were grappling in muddy trenches with the killer Huns, he was dancing the night away with beautiful young ladies. He remembers one night in particular when he and several of his comrades imbibed too much champagne. As punishment, their Wing Lieutenant ordered them to scrub Commander Belmont's floors. Thus the following morning, as ordered, they reported to Commander Belmont's office, brushes and buckets of water in hand.

Puzzled, Belmont looked up from his desk. "What's the meaning of this?"

"Lieutenant's orders, Sir," they responded.

Commander Belmont angrily shook his head. "Men who fly with me in combat do not scrub my floors." He then ordered Skipper and his comrades to return to duty.

Skipper says he entertains fond memories of Commander Belmont till this day. In time he would fly the British Sopwith Camels, the French Nieuports, and, best of all, the U. S. Liberty Plane. His primary duty was to fly high above the German trenches as an observer for American artillery. He also took aerial photographs and participated in early experiments with the "wireless" telephone.

Ben C. Hough, as he appeared in 1976, is surrounded by his momentoes of the Great War. He was trained at Ft. Thomas, Kentucky, then assigned to the 2nd Air Service Mechanics Regiment in France.

Frank Fisher (97th Infantry Division) survived the horrors of World War I, living to celebrate his 106th birthday (above) in 1994.

Another Air Corps veteran Ben C. Hough (1st Company, Motor Division, 2nd Air Corps) was assigned to an aviation company at Issoudun, where he was reunited with his old Lancaster friends, Lee Skipper and Elliott Springs. He also became a close friend of famous American flying ace, Quentin Roosevelt, and says he remembers very vividly the day Roosevelt was killed.

He says that life at Issoudun was perfectly peaceful, except for Big Bertha, the giant artillery piece the Germans used to shell Paris from 75 miles away. "I could hear the BOOM-BOOM at night. During the day we couldn't hear it. But in the stillness of night, it might have been next door."

But most of all, says Hough, he still remembers the sad, demoralized countenances of the poor French civilians. "They had already been in the war for years when we arrived. Actually, there were very few people to be seen—just old men and women, no young people. And they were so helpless. All males between the ages of 17 and 50 were either in the trenches or dead. The war had bled them white.

Coyt Green (27th Infantry Division) recalls his first days in France and the looks of gratitude reflected in the eyes of the British infantry when they first spotted the American Doughboys coming to their aid. (Green explains, by the way, that "Doughboy" was an affectionate nickname the French bestowed upon U.S. soldiers, since the first Americans they met had just completed a long march down a sandy road and were covered from head to foot in a fine, flour-white dust.)

Frank Fisher (97th, "Buffalo" Infantry Division) recalls that the French civilians were "badly beaten, with many starving to death. They used to hang around our garbage cans hoping to find scraps of food." A rifleman in an all-black infantry division, Fisher recounts an interesting

Haskell Bailey (far left) was a cook with Battery C of the 21st Field Artillery. A member of the Occupation Force, Bailey was stationed in Germany when this photograph was taken in May of 1919.

Upon their arrival in France, America's Doughboys rode to either the front or to training centers in these small boxcars called 40 and 8s (they carried 40 men or 8 horses).

Haskell and John Bailey, cousins who served their country diligently, were among the lucky ones who returned to civilian life (and the latest in transportation) in 1919.

story that well illustrates the affection felt by most French civilians for the American soldier:

"It was a dark, foggy night, and we were marching to the front. Somehow, I became separated from my company. I looked around and I realized that I was lost—and of course I was scared of being captured by the Germans. Well, I stumbled around in the dark for what seemed like hours, until finally I came to a little hut in a clearing. I knew I was taking a chance, but I had to get directions. So I knocked. There was a stirring inside, then an elderly Frenchman opened the door. He couldn't underestand me, and I couldn't understand him. But I smiled, and he smiled. He could see that I was an American, and somehow we managed to communicate enough to know that all was well. The man and his wife gave me food, then they gave me a bed. The next morning I was awakened by something hopping around on the bed. Then something wet began nuzzling my face. I jumped up, and there staring me in the eye was a big old red rooster and a little gray donkey. The French kept their animals in the house with them. But they were fine people."

That afternoon Fisher caught up with his company. The next morning they would lead the charge against the Germans at Verdun. Still, Fisher says he's always wondered whatever happened to that kindly French family who saved his life over half a century ago.

Bill Medford says he spent his first night in France near the city of Calais. He, like most of the men of the 30th Division, was quartered temporarily in small round tents.

"SOME WAR," BAILEY WRITES FROM FRANCE

Lancaster Boy Says Though It Is Not So Dreadful as People Imagine.

Miss Dora Bailey, of Lancaster, R. F. D. 6, has received the following letter from her brother, D. L. Bailey, from "Somewhere in France:"

Somewhere at the "Front,"
August 29.

Dear Homepeople:

I suppose I can snatch a few moments just now to write you a brief letter. I could write pages and pages but it would never get by the censor, so you will have to be satisfied with the information that I am in good health, good spirits, and am having a great time. I don't know whether it is permissable to tell how long I have been at the front, but to make sure I shall not tell you. This is the first chance I have had to get any stationary or I would have written you two weeks ago. You will notice that this is Salvation A. paper. I used to almost sneer at the Sal. army but never again will I be guilty of such, and I am pretty sure that after the war there will be few soldiers who ever say anything slight about it. It is right there with the goods, that is for the soldiers at the front. The Y. M. C. A. is good but its service is far better in the training camps and back areas than at the front. I can't give any definite information but you can take it from me that this war is "some war." There is more to it than you people back home ever dreamed of. It is not so dreadful as you may imagine but there are thousands of things that you don't imagine at all. In other words, the word war in the modern sense has a very wide meaning. I'll tell you all about it when I [illegible] back. [illegible] average soldier after being in [illegible] a while never thinks of the [illegible]ument. The last thing to [illegible] er me is the few shells that [illegible] ad sometimes. In fact [illegible] The careless about putting on [illegible] helmets. Don't think that we [illegible] suffering every day and having an awful time. Some day when it is all over we shall never know the difference.

Write me,
L. G. B.

P. S.—I haven't had any mail since I left America.

LICENSE PERSONS FOR [illegible] DISTRIBUTION OF OIL

[illegible] Into Effect October 1 and Persons Coming Within Its Provis-[illegible]

WILL NOT REST UNTIL GERMANY IS DEFEATED

French Ambassador Delivers An Address to Senate When Vases Are Presented It.

Washington, Sept. 26.—Determination of America and the allies to use only the argument of force until Prussian militarism shall have been forever crushed was emphasized in addresses delivered in the senate by Ambassador Jusserand, of France, and Vice-President Marshall. The occasion was the presentation of vases to the senate by the French government in appreciation of the reception accorded the French mission that came to welcome America into the war.

Ambassador Jusserand said the free nations are in the war "until the last gun is fired" so as "to make good for the world the American declaration of independence." Mr. Marshall said America was determined to fight on not only to avenge the wrongs done to France and other nations, but until "Bethlehem shall prevail over Berlin."

A picturesque setting for the presentation ceremonies was given by draping the stars and stripes and the French tri-color on the gallery rails back of the vice-president's rostrum, while below on either side the two huge vases, each nearly six feet tall, were placed in view of the audience, which included members of the diplomatic corps, the house, and other officials. In the galleries were members of the French foreign legion, while friends of the President's family occupied the executive section.

A committee of senators headed by Democratic Leader Martin, of Virginia, and Republican Leader Lodge, of Massachusetts, escorted Ambassador Jusserand to the rotrum beside Mr. Marshall.

In closing his address the ambassador spoke feelingly of the unusual honor accorded him in being given the privilege of addressing the senate.

Addresses of both Ambassador Jusserand and the vice-president were received with unusual demonstration, the senate rules against applause being suspended. After the ceremonies the ambassador, vice-president, and members of the senate, flanked by the gifts of the French government, were photographed on the capitol portico.

WOMAN SUFFRAGE NOW IS ON THE DEFENSIVE

Facing Almost Certain Defeat the Supporters Are "At Sea" as to Next Step.

Washington, Sept. 30.—With certain defeat or withdrawal admitted to be the only present alternative the house resolution proposing submission to the States of the Susan B. Anthony equal suffrage amendment furnished another sharp, but brief, fight in the senate Saturday and then went over until today. In the meantime conferences were held between its supporters to decide whether on Monday it shall be brought to a vote with defeat apparently assured, or again be laid aside indefinitely.

Facing a filibuster begun by opponents of the resolution, loss of the vote of Senator Benet of South Carolina who had been counted among the supporters but who announced he would vote in the negative, and also absence of many senators supporting the resolution, the woman suffrage forces were on the defensive. That the opposition is strong enough to defeat the resolution was conceded both by Senators Pittman, of

On August 29, 1918, D. L. Bailey wrote the above letter to his sister Dora Bailey. It was published in The Lancaster News on September 20th. (The author regrets the poor condition of older copies of the Lancaster News.*)*

Thomas Vance Bailey was inducted in June of 1918 and discharged in December, some six months later. He was assigned to the 8th Regiment, Field Artillery, at Camp Jackson. The war ended before he was exposed to the horrors of combat.

"First, we dug a hole, then the tent was put up around the hole. then sandbag barricades were erected outside the tent as protection against shrapnel." Actually, adds Medford, it was a great deal of work for nothing, because every time a German plane flew over he and his friends would dash from their shelter to watch the exploding bombs and try to catch sight of their first real "German aeroplane." (This is the same Bill Medford, you'll recall, who raced up on deck to watch for torpedo attacks.)

Except for the nightly bombings, life for the average Lancaster soldier wasn't too difficult at this point. Before very much longer they would fight for their very lives at such places as Ypres, the Somme, the Marne, Chateau-Thierry, Belleau Wood, Verdun, the Hindenburg Line, Burgundy, and Metz. But during their first weeks in France our soldiers would hike the two miles to Calais in the evenings and visit with young ladies, tour the city, or sit for hours in one of Calais' many beer gardens.

"In fact," laughs Bill Medford, "if the Americans saw any combat their first weeks in France, it was against the British soldiers in the beer gardens of Calais and Brest. We had little use for the British or French soldiers, especially the British. They were snobs who made no secret of the fact that they found us ill-bred, and that attitude sort of rubbed us the wrong way. Later, when combat did come, it was the Colonial troops who won our respect—the Austrailians, Canadians, and the Scotch. They were the real fighters in World War I."

And W.C. Bowers (114th Machinegun Battalion, 81st Infantry Division) adds: "The French civilians were fine, but the French soldiers didn't like us at all. They were jealous of us, you see, because it was rumored that we dated their wives and sweethearts while they were off at the front. And to a certain extent, I guess they were right."

While most of our troops underwent months of training after reaching France, a few were forced to face the stark realities of war almost immediately. Frank Fisher, for example, and his 97th Infantry Division were thrown into combat within a week of their arrival in France. He recalls that they were packed into boxcars called "forty and eights" (forty men or eight horses), and then taken to within marching distance of the front lines. "There were no first class passengers in those cars," he laughs. "For each car of forty men the army supplied a case of stewed tomatoes and forty loaves of bread. When that was gone we did without until we had a chance to re-supply, which might be two or three days."

F.H. Adams remembers that his company was moved up to the front after only a week of training. He recalls marching for days on end, then one day they came upon a little church standing in a wooded area. Darkness was approaching, but they could see that the church's steeple had been shot away while the church itself remained undamaged.

"We were ordered inside to bed down for the night. So I spread my blanket out and prepared to go to sleep on that cold stone floor. We were dead tired, and we had just stretched out when the captain came in and said, 'Pack up, men, and move outside. The Germans have us in their sights and plan to shell us before dawn.' Well, we went outside and got in formation. Then the captain said, 'Men, I've just been handed an order. We're moving up to the front line trenches.' Well, I felt a chill run through me at this, and so did everyone else. Just then, a young friend of mine from North Carolina, his name was Bob and he was just a kid of 17 and I'd sort of taken him under my wing and was looking out for him. Well, at that point Bob broke ranks and ran back inside the church. Then we heard a shot. Some of us went in to see what was wrong, and Bob had blown his head off. We found his body lying there with his rifle beside him. He'd pulled the trigger with his toe."

Before war's end, Adams would see thousands of men killed at the front, but he would never forget his young friend committing suicide on the eve of battle.

H.M. Robinson (322nd Regiment, 81st Infantry Division) was another of our soldiers thrown immediately into combat. After a rough crossing of the

J.P. Richards (right) took basic training at Camp Sevier, then was among the first Americans to go to France as a member of the 30th Infantry Division. At the Hindenburg Line, he recieved a battlefield commission for bravery under fire. In later life he would be elected to the U.S. Senate.

Hartsell M. Robinson (far right) stands with friends Jim Watts of Camden and Frank Helten of Jefferson. All served with Company F, 322nd Regiment, 81st Infantry Division, and all were immediately thrown into combat once they arrived in France in July 1918.

ary, Cabinet Mem-
e, to Avoid Mob
This Country.

TTING SERIOUS

siness Sidetracked
iation of Disloy-
on, German Spies
. W.

April 8.—All other
id aside by the sen-
denunciation of dis-
, German spies and
nd discussion of how
t should be extended
hese evils and avoid
t abridging the fun-
es of American citi-

senate debated the
bill, carrying se-
r disloyel utterances
obstruct the draft or
President Wilson and
attention to reports
of Robert Prague, a
ollinsville, Ill., last
s of the cabinet said
deplorable incident
necessity for imme-
that would enable
to deal with disloy-
agitation so that the
t be tempted to take
eir own hands.
n leaders in the sen-
the sedition bill, the
America's entrance
An agreement for a
Senator Overman, in
measure, was blocked
ed. The Missouri
was in sympathy
l purposes of the leg-
ught it should not be
ed. When Senator
that the attorney
rged passage of the
provisions would be
he Liberty loan cam-
Reed said that was
e."
iscussion, the attitude
r, socialist candidate
n the recent Wiscon-
s denounced by Sen-
d Lodge, as disloyal
treason.
e, while urging the
or spies and German
stroy property in this
the bill's restrictions

Weekly War Review Summarizes Operations Along the Western Front.

HUN PLANS WERE FOILED

Prisoners Taken Say That the Kaiser's Troops Expected to Gain the Line of the Somme on First Day.

Washington, April 8.—French and British tenacity has upset the ambitious plans of the German high command for the battle of Picardy, says the war department's weekly military review, and now the enemy, determined to gain some sort of success at any cost, is throwing fresh forces into the battle in an effort to secure limited objectives. Because of this, the situation is expected to remain uncertain for sometime to come.

General improvement in the strategic positions of the allies is noted, and the review declares that under General Foch the allied military machine is working smoothly and efficiently in stemming the German assault.

There is no mention whatever of the American troops reported hurrying to the front to join the British and French.

Enemy Still Short.

"At the opening of the tihr week of the German offensive, we find that the enemy is still short of attaining his principal objectives," says the review in part.

"It is now certain that the German high command contemplated overwhelming the British at the outset, between the Oise and the Sensee and driving a wadge into the Franco-British forces.

"The enemy fully expected to achieve a decision in the field in the course of one great battle. The success of this plan depended on being able to obtain a break-through of the British front and advance so rapidly that neither the French nor the British reserves could come up in time to close the breach in the line.

What Germany Hoped.

"Evidence of prisoners tend to confirm that the enemy hoped to gain the line of the Somme by the evening of the first day of the offensive. As a matter of fact it took the

REPRESENTED BY STARS.

The names of the boys, formerly students of Central School, represented by stars on the service flag presented to the school by the people of the city last Wednesday, are as follows:

JOHN HILLIARD,
ELLIOTT SPRINGS,
LEE SKIPPER,
GEORGE FAIREY POOVEY,
HERMAN POOVEY,
JULIAN ROSS,
LEIGHTON HORTON,
BOYD HORTON,
WALTER BEATY,
GARY ELLIOTT,
THUDUS FAILE,
JETHER FAILE,
RODDEY BELL,
MALLIE FERGUSON,
W. B. CAUTHEN, Jr.,
PAUL ROSS MOORE,
WILL ROSS MOORE,
CANTZEN MOORE,
FOSTER MOORE,
JOE COULBOURNE,
STEVE WILLIAMS,
WALTER McMANUS,
BEN C. HOUGH,
BEVAN FUNDERBURK,
PIERCE HORTON,
STRAIT PARKS,
HACKER BILLINGS,
STAFFORD GRAHAM,
LEE McDOW,
ROBERT BECKHAM,
CARL BENNETT,
LUCIUS BENNETT,
FRED BLACKMON,
ELMER SOWELL,
ROSCOE LINGLE,
FRED ADAMS,
W. F. STOLL,
CRAWFORD CULP,
R. THOS. BEATY,
STANLEY WILLIAMSON,
ORRIN C. BLACKMON,
W. J. MONTGOMERY,
CHARLIE COOK,
HOYT HUNTER,
REID FERGUSON,
ELVIN SNIPES,
SAMUEL MOTHERSHED,
LEONARD HUDSON,
EDWARD P. MONTGOMERY,
WILL JOHNSON,
FRANK MOON BOLDRIDGE,
AUSTIN BOLDRIDGE,
JOHN REID BOLDRIDGE,
CHAUNCEY BOLDRIDGE,
FURMAN HINSON,
MORRIS McILWAINE,
WILSON MOSIER,
W. B. CAUTHEN.

CALLS
OF GE
FORC

President
Says Ar
"Forc

WITHOU

"The Righ
Force W
the La
Cast E
Down i

Baltimor
Wilson's ac
Saturday
lenege that
central po
settled by
sons cheeri
The Pr
plainly wit
of German
applauded
ready at a
peace since
The Pre
nothing is
justice was
his stateme
in Russia i
Force M
When th
he accept
and that fo
the audien
cheered for
Former
borough in
declared th
come a ne
erty. Mr.
can, said th
try must ra
"This is
borough,
ment. Th
body to get
At the c
dent's add
opened for
ings Bank
took $1,00
amounts w
In full, t

On April 9, 1918, the Lancaster News *announced that a flag would be presented to the Central School bearing a star for each of its graduates now in service.*

Atlantic in a Kennedy Cattle Boat, his outfit arrived at Brest only to be told that 40 volunteers were needed to bolster a certain defensive line. When no one stepped forward, a French officer briskly marched down the first rank of American soldiers, tapping them on the chest with his riding crop as he walked. They were the "volunteers." And Robinson was among them. He would later be credited with singlehandedly capturing 11 German soldiers who were out on a midnight scouting mission.

But for the majority of our soldiers, especially those men of the 27th and 30th Divisions, their first encounter with the Germans would come just outside a small Belgian city in July 1917. This battle would last from July until November, and would go down in the history books as the Third Battle of Ypres (Passchendaele). In the end nothing was gained and the Americans and British suffered a combined total of 245,000 casualties.

Oscar Roddy Bell remembers that the 30th Infantry Division departed Calais and crossed the Belgian border at exactly eight a.m. on the morning of July 4, 1917. They marched on then for another three hours before approaching a dark muddy encampment in a wooded area known as "The Dirty Bucket," just to the rear of the front line trenches. Then they just sat and waited. He could hear huge shells exploding near by, then a dead British soldier was brought in on a stretcher. Bell watched anxiously as the British officer in charge of burial details knelt by the stretcher and ripped open the dead boy's shirt. He then opened a small pouch that hung around the dead boy's neck by a string, and counted out 33 cents. This, Bell learned, was to pay the British government for the army blanket the boy was to be buried in, a general practice in the British army.

Ira Harper (seated in chair) and an unidentified friend tug playfully at a bottle of cognac. This photograph was taken in Paris several weeks following the Armistice when everyone, following a year of horror, was in a playful mood. Harper was assigned to the American Motor School in Sathonay from August 1918 until his discharge in May 1919.

Today Bell shakes his head sadly. "Our nerves were stretched pretty taunt anyway, and seeing all that did nothing to make us feel any better. We ourselves went into the trenches that afternoon."

Bill Medford remembers Ypres as a great sea of mud and desolation. He recalls standing in a trench anxiously watching the German army. Their trenches were only 200 yards away, he says, and he remembers that the Germans were doing the same, standing in their trenches watching the Americans. Soon they were waving back and forth

ARMY SONG BOOK

For free distribution to all
Officers and Men in the Army

Issued by the War Department Commission on Training Camp Activities and compiled with the assistance of the National Committee on Army and Navy Camp Music

WASHINGTON
1918

This U.S. Army songbook was carried by Ira Harper in France.

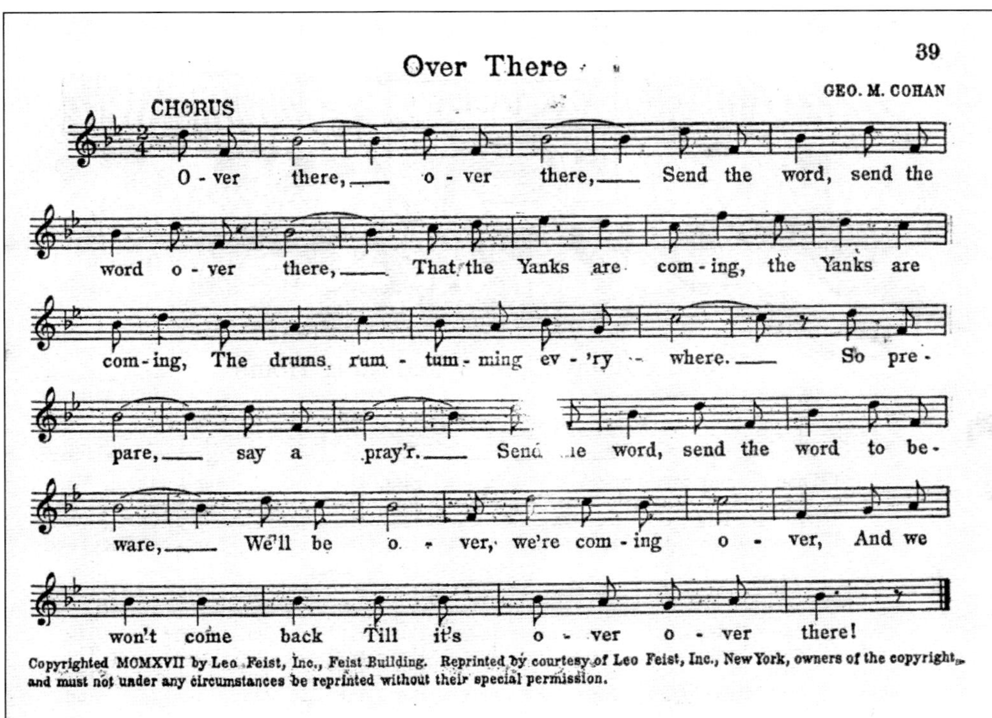

to each other, a diversion that seemed to delight boys from both sides.

That night, however, the picture changed considerably, as the darkness was coninually shattered by exploding artillery bursts. This practice became a nightly affair, says Medford, and soon his sector of the front became known as Hell's Fire Corner. He still has fond memories of the brave Scotch troops who alternated front line duty with his company.

"They were magnificient, those Scottish troops, marching in just at sundown, all in line, all in step with their bagpipes, as though they were on parade back in Scotland. They wore these fancy colored kilts, and high socks bearing their regimental colors. I've never seen such a memorable sight."

Ypres meant a close brush with death for W.B. Adams. "We had not been at the front for an hour when we came upon an old shelled-out farm house. And behind it stood an old barn. I said to myself, 'If there is a sniper around here,

Charles S. Caskey took basic training at Camp Jackson before being assigned to the 302nd Guard and Fire Company, Quartermaster Corps, in Jersey City, New Jersey. He was aboard a troop transport ship bound for France when the war ended on November 11, 1918.

38

On the Way to France

Words by
HOMER HOWELLS HARBOUR

Melody "Marche Lorraine"

Here's an army of the Yankees
On the way to France;
Here's an army of the Yankees
On the way to France;
From New England down to Texas
We are marching on to join the Great Advance,
On the way to France.

From New England down to Texas
On the way to France;
From New England down to Texas
On the way to France,
There's a million men in khaki
Drilling day and night to make the Prussians dance
Over there in France.

There's a million men in khaki
On the way to France;
There's a million men in khaki,
On the way to France,
Who will join the gallant armies
Of our noble Allies in their Great Advance
Over there in France?

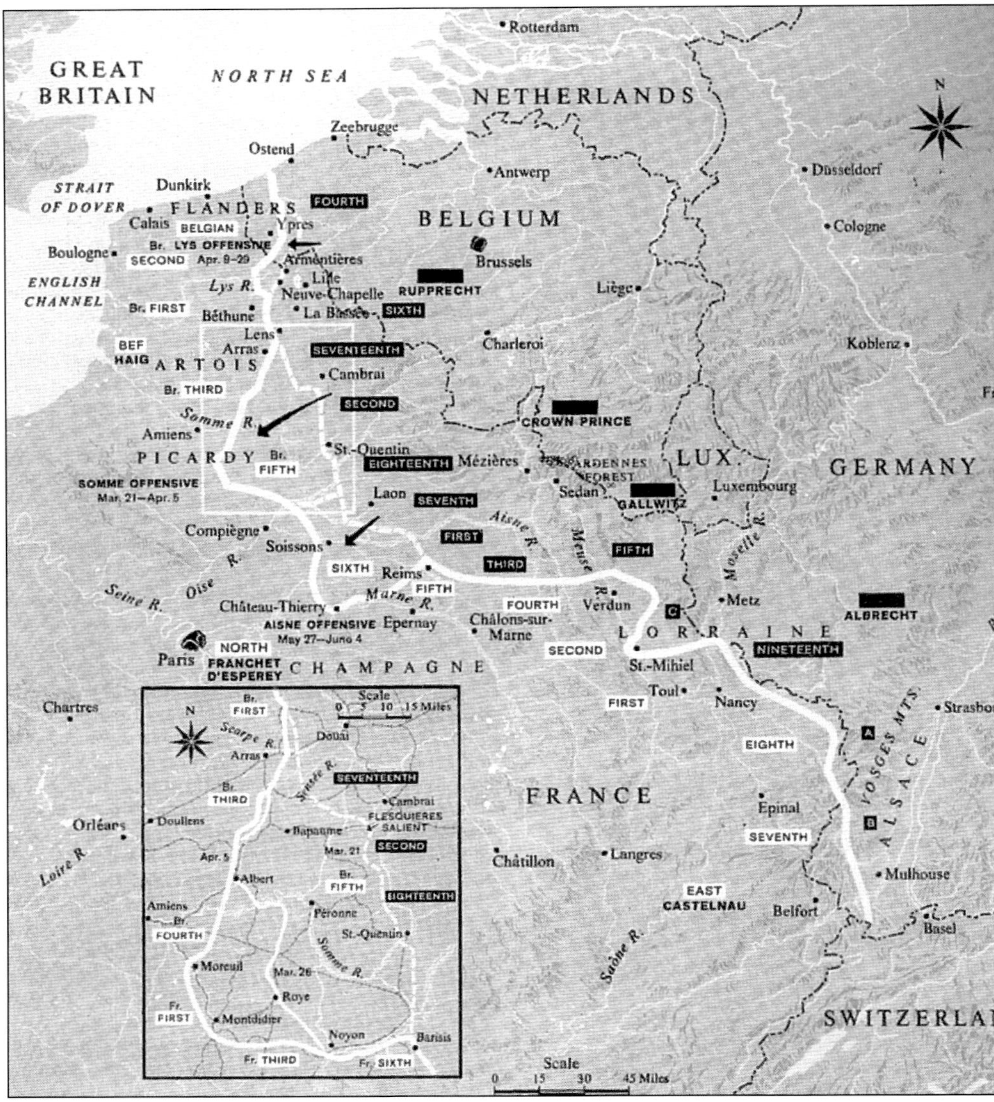

that would be a good place for him to hide.' Well, bless God, I had no more thought that when a bullet whizzed by, clipping the front rim off my helmet. Our lieutenant yelled, 'Keep your head down or you'll be killed.' Then all the fellows started firing and that old barn seemed to fly apart—timber flying everywhere. Then the sniper tumbled out of the upstairs opening. We went over and looked at him. He was dead, his body riddled with bullets. Just a kid, really, looked about 15. I felt bad about him then. But after a while you get hardened to it. You get to the place where you'd just as soon die as live, and you're not really a good soldier until you do."

Roland Lattimore, also a member of the 30th Division, presents a vivid picture of life down in the trenches on the eve of battle.

"They kept us way under ground in what we called a dugout for several days before we went into battle. One day a sergeant and I were standing guard at the entrance to our dugout to keep anyone from trying to slip out.

There was a big siren which would go off if we wanted to alert everyone to some danger. Well, I was on guard that afternoon, which was to be our first day of combat, and some colonels came up and said they wanted to see our company commander. Well, I knew something was up, you know, so I kept my eyes open. And in a little while our commander came out, and I asked him if we were going into battle. He didn't say anything, he just looked at me like he was in shock. Then he said, 'Go in and roll your pack—but keep it quiet.'

"So I went down into the dugout and lit the candle by my bunk and started getting my things together. The other fellows roused up and were curious, and they all got up and said, 'Lat, what you doing that for?' And I could hear the fear in their voices.

"I just said, 'Don't worry, you'll get your orders soon enough.'

"They said, 'You're rolling your pack to go to the front, aren't you.' Well, I couldn't tell them, but they knew. They turned white as cotton. And sure enough, we went up front to the trenches

Since his only military experience to date had been gained in an army hospital, Joe Gandy was assigned to work as a medic in Base Hospital #78 once he arrived in France.

KEEP THIS CARD
S. S. CZARITZA
Third
YOU WILL MESS IN ~~SECOND~~
CLASS DINING ROOM
SECOND SITTING

Above is Ira Harper's meal ticket from when he returned home aboard the S.S. Czaritza *in 1919.*

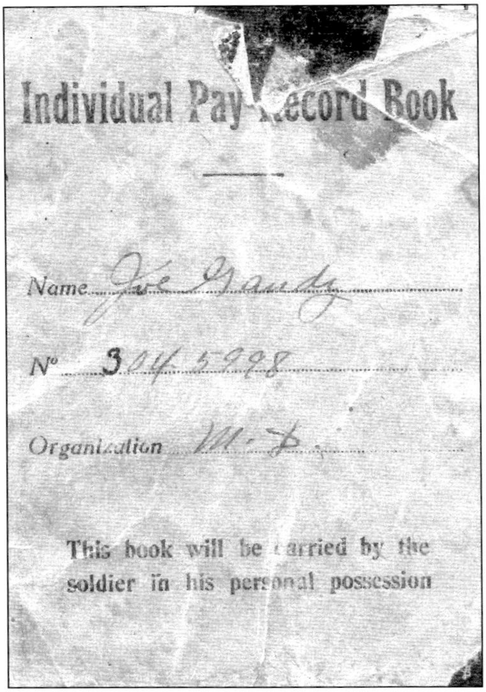

Individual Pay Record Book

Name Joe Gandy

No. 3045998

Organization M.D.

This book will be carried by the soldier in his personal possession

These two images show the Individual Pay Record Book carried by Joe Gandy in France. In addition to free room and board down in the trenches, he was also paid the grand sum of $36.00 per month.

just before dawn of the next day. Some 12 hours later we'd driven the Germans out of three different towns."

Lattimore goes on to say, "There were times at the front when we were face-to-face with the Germans, but there were so many of them, swarming from all over, that we really couldn't tell who killed who. I would see them fall, but I didn't know whether I'd done it or not. But the worst thing was when they'd come at us with their bayonets, and they'd be blowing these shrill police whistles. That's when our hearts would pound and we'd start shooting like crazy people. But really, we couldn't stand it long in the front lines. Three days was about as long as anyone could take it without losing his mind."

As for food, getting a hot meal at the front was considered nearly impossible. The men just opened a can of whatever was available, if anything, and hoped for the best. Otherwise, recalls J.P. Richards (30th Infantry Division), their daily fare consisted almost totally of stewed corned beef, what the men referred to as "corn willy." Since then, adds

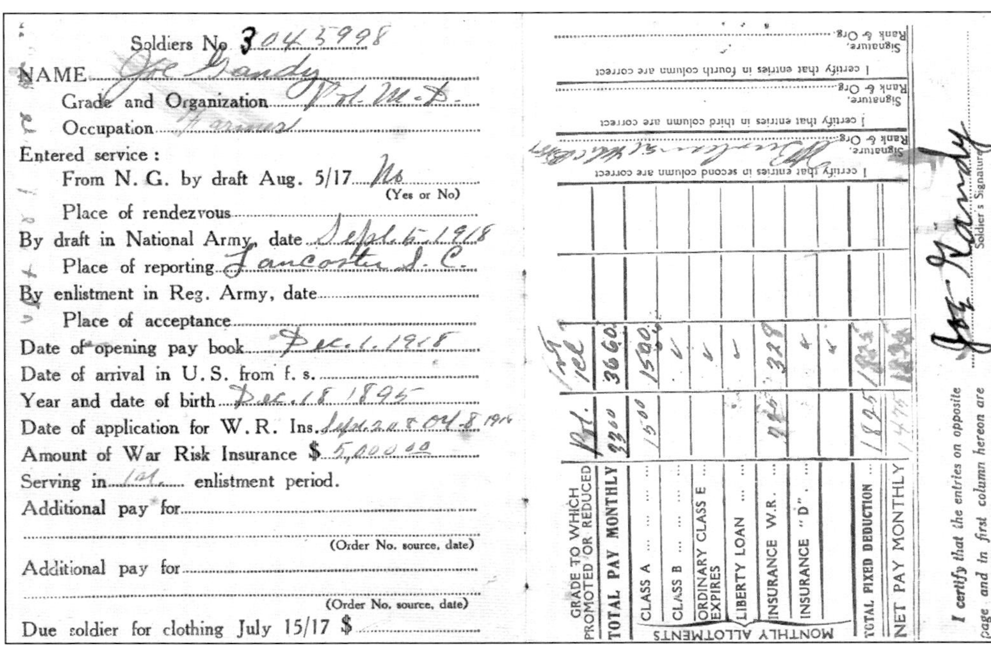

Soldiers No. 3045998

NAME Joe Gandy

Grade and Organization Pvt. M.D.

Occupation Farmer

Entered service:

From N. G. by draft Aug. 5/17 No (Yes or No)

Place of rendezvous

By draft in National Army, date Sept. 5 1918

Place of reporting Lancaster S. C.

By enlistment in Reg. Army, date

Place of acceptance

Date of opening pay book Dec. 1. 1918

Date of arrival in U. S. from f. s.

Year and date of birth Dec. 18 1895

Date of application for W. R. Ins. Sept. 20 & Oct. 8 1918

Amount of War Risk Insurance $ 5,000.00

Serving in 1st enlistment period.

Additional pay for (Order No. source, date)

Additional pay for (Order No. source, date)

Due soldier for clothing July 15/17 $

GRADE TO WHICH PROMOTED OR REDUCED	Pvt.	
TOTAL PAY MONTHLY	33.00	36.00
MONTHLY ALLOTMENTS: CLASS A	15.00	15.00
CLASS B		
ORDINARY CLASS E EXPIRES		
LIBERTY LOAN		
INSURANCE W.R.	3.25	3.28
INSURANCE "D"		
TOTAL FIXED DEDUCTION	18.25	18.28
NET PAY MONTHLY	14.75	

I certify that entries in second column are correct. Signature. Rank & Org.

I certify that entries in third column are correct. Signature. Rank & Org.

I certify that entries in fourth column are correct. Signature. Rank & Org.

I certify that the entries on opposite page and in first column hereon are correct.

Joe Gandy

Soldier's Signature

Richards, he has avoided corned beef whenever possible.

Of course, if the men were hungry enough, and generally they were, they would eat anything. Howard K. Williamson recalls making a long forced march to relieve the beleaguered 97th Division, whose ranks had been decimated by the Germans. For three days and nights they marched through knee deep mud, strafed by German planes, shelled by artillery from both sides, and almost starved to death. Then, Williamson remembers, sometime during the small hours of the third night, a supply wagon came rolling up. A quart sized can was tossed down in his lap. "That's for your squad," the supply man called and drove away. A few moments later a sharp-eyed sergeant dropped down beside him.

"What you got in that can?" he whispered so as not to waken the men sleeping around them.

Williamson read the label. It was grape jelly.

The sergeant gave his ribs a sharp nudge. "Come on, let's eat it."

Williamson shook his head. "Can't. It's for my squad."

"I don't give a damn for your squad," snarled the sergeant. He pointed to the three stripes on his sleeve. "You see them stripes? Well, I'm telling you, I got a loaf of bread and you got a can of jelly. So you get that can open and let's start eating. And that's an order!"

For the next 30 minutes, recalls Williamson, he and his new friend then sat quietly in the darkness and contentedly consumed the entire loaf of bread and about a pint of jelly. (Williamson says that in hopes of avoiding a mass mutiny, he neglected to mention this episode to his squad.)

Roland Lattimore remembers living in the muddy front line trenches for three days, eating whatever was available, when his captain informed him one morning that a field kitchen had been set up two miles to their rear. Lattimore then collected 10 men to help bring back rations and set off for the kitchen, visions of roast turkey dancing in his mind. He knew his company was moving out, but the captain told him that a private would be left behind to point them in the right direction once they'd returned with the food.

Sgt. Coke Bridges and Cpl. G. Otis Mobley, were both natives of Heath Springs and both members of Company L, 118th Regiment, 30th Infantry Division. They were among the first Americans to arrive in France.

He and the other 10 had just arrived at the kitchen and picked up their rations, he says, when he felt the whole world begin to tremble. "My God," he thought, "they've set up another barrage."

and New Hope Sunday schools will be held Sunday, September 1 for the benefit of the entire community. The services will be held at New Hope at 10 a. m. and at Oak Ridge at 3 p. m. Everybody invited to attend.

—o—

Voting Was Lively.

The voting at the Lancaster precinct today was quite lively, about 150 votes having been cast at ten o'clock this morning. The Australian ballot was used for the first time and four booths were prepared for the use of the voters, only four being allowed within the enclosure at one time.

—o—

Piedmont Springs Hotel Burns.

The Piedmont Springs hotel, a popular summer resort three miles east of King's Creek, was destroyed by fire Thursday afternoon about one o'clock. The building was a two-story structure containing 40 rooms. Practically all the contents were consumed. The hotel was owned by a party of Gaffney men and was managed by R. J. Castles.

—o—

Calls for More Men.

The local board has received calls, in addition to that for Thursday of this week, for five white men on August 30 to Camp Green, three negroes on September 1 to Camp Jackson, 40 white men on September 3 to Camp Jackson, and 10 "limited service" men on September 6 to Camp Greenleaf, Ga. These calls will be filled from class 1 of the 1918 registration.

—o—

Dragging the Streets.

The city authorities have had a force of workmen engaged this week in dragging the streets, especially North Main from the asphalt pavement at the court house to the foot of the hill. The streets would now be in much better condition if a rain should come to settle the dust, and if the workmen would pick up the rocks and bottles dragged from the ditches.

—o—

PERSONALS.

R. A. Williams, of the Creek section, returned Saturday from Charleston to vote in the primary.

—o—

Assistant Attorney General Claud N. Sapp, of Columbia, was here today to vote in the primary. He left for Columbia on the afternoon train.

—o—

Mr. and Mrs. R. R. Riddle and

FORTY-THREE MEN OFF FOR CAMP THURSDAY

These Go to Camp Jackson and Takes Last Man in Class 1 of the 1917 Registration.

The following men have been called by the local board, 43 of whom will entrain for Camp Jackson Thursday morning. This call wipes out class 1 of the 1917 registration and re-classification and future calls will be filled from the 1918 class.

Adam B. Heglar, Kershaw, R. 2.
Albert T. Hinson, Lancaster, R. 1.
John R. Lowry, Taxahaw.
Grover C. Craig, Jefferson.
Albert Haire, Lancaster, R. 2.
Luke Phillips, Lancaster.
Sam D. Furr, Lancaster, R. 6.
Edgar M. Bowers, Heath Springs.
James Cauthen, Lancaster R. 6.
Melvin W. Faile, Taxahaw.
Luther Eubanks, Kershaw, R. 5.
Ernest B. Lucas, Kershaw, R. 3.
Otis Robinson, Lancaster.
Charlie N. McClintock, Riverside, R. F. D.
Elmer Cauthen, Lancaster.
Melvin W. Cauthen, Heath Springs, R. 2.
Ben F. Usher, Lancaster, R. 2.
Roland Beaver, Lancaster.
Ben Stacks, Tradesville.
Lee C. Craig, Lancaster.
Joe C. Vickery, Osceola, R. 1.
Hazel A. Funderburk, Tradesville.
Ben Adams, Kershaw, R. 5.
Chester Neal, Lancaster, R. 1.
George Robinson, Kershaw, R. 5.
Bishop B. Courtney, Waxhaw.
Marion Sims, Kershaw, R. 3.
Hoyt Dees, Heath Springs.
George Raley, Osceola, R. 1.
Cull Hunter, Lancaster.
Herney Harris, Lancaster.
Geo. W. Parr, Lancaster.
Earl H. Beck, Lancaster.
John W. Evans, Lancaster.
Clyde S. Stogner, Lancaster, R. 6.
Fred M. Wright, Kershaw, R. 2.
Henry Wilson, Lancaster.
Wilbert Langley, Lancaster.
William H. Hester, Lancaster, R. 8
William G. Funderburk, Tradesville.
James B. Ellis, Waxhaw, R. 5.
John Stevens, Kershaw, R. 3.
Robert Craig, Taxahaw, R. 2.
H. R. Roberts, Lancaster.
Robert W. Coleman, Lancaster.
Ernest Sims, Lancaster.
Frank Maree, Lancaster.
Hurley Baker, Lancaster.
Thos. F. Baker, Lancaster.
Willie G. Strait, Lancaster.

ference. The field agents decided that the only way in which the needed laborers could be secured was to take them from non-essential industry.

"The time has come for the entire nation to realize that business as usual is no longer possible," Nathan A. Smyth, assistant director of the employment service told the conference. "If we are to end the war quickly the production of luxuries and non-essentials in this country must come to an end. It is a question of winning the war quickly or having it drag on indefinitely.

"Manufacturers must give up the creation of needless goods, workers must be willing to change from non-essential to war production even at a hardship to themselves; the public at large must stop buying luxuries and thereby make the problem of curtailing non-essentials easier.'

Following are the industries which the district board, the first to make an announcement, has held as non-essential:

Auto industry accessories, drivers of pleasure cars, cleaning, repairing and delivery of same, sight seeing cars, auto trucks other than those hauling fuel or doing government work, teaming other than delivery of products for war work; bath and barber shop attendants; bowling, billiard and pool rooms, bottlers and bottle supplies, candy manufacturers and delicatenessn establishments, builders and contractors not engaged in erection of structures for war work; dancing academies, mercantile stores; florists; fruit stands; junk dealers; livery and sales stables; pawn brokers; peanut venders, shoe shining shops, window cleaners, sofe drink establishments, soda fountain supplies.

HOLD CONSULTATION MEET IN COLUMBIA

(Continued From Page One.)

and are good drivers will be accepted. Thousands of nurses' aids are being called for France. The American women are being asked to take their places beside those of the English and French women.

In the coming Christmas drive for membership, it is hoped that every person in every country will become a member of the Red Cross, not only for the help that it will give the Red Cross, but for the effect on the enemy of a large Red Cross membership. New attractive posters, signs and badges will be sent out.

The Red Cross Nurse.

Miss Van De Vrede spoke next

The army's need for men was insatiable, and on May 24, 1918, the Lancaster News *announced that still more young men were to be called up. These were to meet at the court house before departing for various camps on May 28th.*

He explains, "Down in the trenches, we were between these two fields of fire, our artillery and the German artillery. Both sides were firing over us, and the shells were dropping here and there, a great many of them dropping right on us. And it looked like the whole world was being churned up, and the shrapnel was flying all over the place, whizzing right over our heads.

"So we grabbed our rations and began running back towards our trenches, big sacks of food slung over our shoulders, and we finally made it back. And sure enough, we found that our company had already moved out. So there we were, big sacks of food slung over our shoulders, wondering what to do. We had loaves of bread, cans of tomatoes and other goods, and I was just standing there wondering what to do. The private the captain had left behind to guide us was suffering from shell shock and couldn't say a word. He was just sitting there in the mud beside our trench, holding his head in his hands and shaking all over. He kept saying over and over, 'The sky is so blue. The sky is so blue.'

"Well, there we were trying to decide what to do, wondering where we were and where the Germans were, when an artillery round came roaring in. So we all dived for bottom of the trench—all but the poor boy who was suffering from shock. Moments later we peeped over the top of our trench and from the look of what we saw, that shell must have landed right in the poor boy's lap. We got our rations, but it cost that boy his life. But that's the way combat was. Whether you lived or died had nothing to do with how good or how bad you were, but just on where you happened to be standing at the moment."

Ira Harper, an artilleryman assigned to a replacement depot, recalls that his happiest experience of the war occurred not long after his arrival in France while helping unload a supply ship.

John T. Bennett was inducted in July 1917, received basic training at Camp Jackson, then was shipped overseas in May of 1918. Assigned to the 699th Motor Transport Company, he saw action as a medic in France, Belgium, and Italy. He returned to Charleston in March 1919 aboard the Mercury.

"Well, it was a terribly hot morning in August, and we'd been hungry ever since we'd left New York, but this morning the officer in charge said we could eat anything we wanted—as long as he didn't see us do it. He didn't look, of course, and we ate about as much as we unloaded that day, about as much as we ordinarily ate in a month."

Oscar Roddy Bell (118th Regiment, 30th Infantry Divison) was among the first boys to report for duty in September of 1917. He was gassed and left for dead at the Hindenburg Line.

In addition to the Germans and an uncertain supply line, our men also had another enemy to contend with, the huge rats that converged by the millions on the muddy, corpse-strewn battlefields of France. The men thought of them as hideous ghouls and shuddered at the sight of them.

W.B. Adams frowns and says: "The rats would eat you alive. I kept my rations, what they call hardtack, in my pack. And I'd been in the front line trenches for two days and nights, and when I was relieved I crawled back to one of the rear trenches to get some sleep. I laid my pack down, then settled down with my head resting on it, using it as sort of a pillow, you know. Well, when I woke up the next morning, the rats had chewed through my pack, through all my clothing, and had devoured every crumb of my hardtack. They were really vicious."

And Ben C. Hough recalls: "As we advanced through France, we used to sleep in the trenches abandoned by the Germans. I was just about asleep one night when I felt something sting my finger. I looked down and the biggest rat I'd ever seen was trying with all his might to rip my finger off. I'm not joking, he was as big as a cat. See, the trenches were about four feet deep, and there was lattice work on the bottom for us to walk on. Of course everything was mud, and water was always under the lattice work. Those rats would burrow down in the mud and hide. Sometimes they'd get in our packs and we'd carry them around for days. I still have a scar where that rat bit me.

"This is terrible to mention, but there were always men being killed out in what we called No Man's Land, the area between the American and German trenches, where no one could get to 'em to bring 'em in. And after only a couple of days of lying out there, there'd be nothing left of those corpses but skeletons. The rats would come from everywhere and eat the rest. But as hard and cynical as we became after a few months at the front, that was something we never talked about—the fact that we could wind up as nothing more than food for the rats. It was too horrible to contemplate."

As the grim winds of winter swept across France in 1918, our men found themselves confronted by another enemy: the terrible cold for which most were ill prepared or equipped.

H.M. Robinson remembers his unit making the big push up Dead Man Hill in the Argonne Forest. Facing his regiment, he says, was a horseshoe of battle-hardened German infantry and

artillery. For a while the battle went well, but then, with American casualties beginning to mount in the face of withering fire from the entrenched Germans, our boys began to fall back. Robinson joined the general retreat, literally running for his life, he says, and he remembers hurdling a shallow shell crater. When he hit the ground the skin of his feet and legs burst open. They were frozen stiff. Unable now to run, he became an easy target for German gunners and his body was ripped by 13 machinegun bullets before he could crawl to shelter. As a result of these wounds, he would spend the next two months in an English hospital. Then he was once again returned to the front.

Roland Lattimore remembers the cold of France as more intense than anything he'd ever experienced in the Carolinas. He recalls Verdun and his company engaging the Germans in heavy combat throughout the day. That night, with artillery shell exploding all about him, he wearily dropped down behind a shattered tree trunk. With his breath coming in gasps from fear and exhaustion, he unscrewed the cap of his canteen, then greedily tilted it upwards. But nothing happened. The water inside was frozen solid. It would be another 12 hours before he could stop long enough to thaw it out.

But the enemy our men most dreaded was poison gas. Bill Medford recalls that there were machines designed specifically for the release of this gas (either chlorine or mustard). But, says Medford, if the wind happened to shift directions, the gas would be blown back in your own face. Therefore, in order to avoid gassing yourself, the gas was generally fired at the enemy in canisters, like artillery shells.

John T. Bennett (third from left) stands with members of his company from France. One of these men drove the car in the background for a local army hospital.

Coyt Green was merely one of thousands of American soldiers who fell beneath this deadly cloud. Because of his small size (he now weighed only a little over 100 pounds), he was made a messenger once he arrived in France, running communiques from company to company, usually under fire. He recalls starting out under the cover of darkness one night to deliver an important message to Division Headquarters, which was situated several miles to the rear, when a sudden artillery barrage prompted him to seek shelter in what appeared to be an old bombed out factory of some sort. Once inside, he says, he looked around and noted with some alarm that he was not alone. There, propped up around what remained of the walls, wrapped in their gray wool blankets, were some 200 other soldiers, all sleeping soundly. For the next hour they remained motionless, and Green wondered how anyone could sleep at a time like that.

It was not until the shelling ended that he discovered the reason for their imperturbable calm. He crept quietly over to the nearest sleeping soldier and slowly lifted the corner of the blanket from the soldier's face. Then he jumped back in horror. His sleeping compannions were all dead, he discovered, the corpses which his division had tagged that day and placed in the old mill to await burial. Green staggered from the factory.

He had not gone very far, however, when he heard someone shout, "Gas!" and men began dropping like flies. Before he could get his gas mask out of its pouch, he too collapsed. But by some miracle he didn't die. Instead, he was picked up and shipped to a hospital in London, where he lay in a coma for three weeks. He was then returned to the front.

Oscar Roddy Bell remembers being gassed and taken to an army hospital in Rouen. "It was there," he says, "that I saw the real horrors of war—the worst being those who'd been burned with mustard gas. Some were blind, some were without lips and ears. They looked like someone had poured scalding water on their faces."

Bell then went on to relate the following inspirational story: "But talk about courage and perseverance, I've never seen anyone as brave as John Faulkenberry. John was a great big fellow and when we were in basic training they couldn't find a pair of shoes big enough to fit him, so they told him he could just go on back home. But John refused to leave. Instead, he took his knife and cut the sides out of the shoes they'd given him. Then later in France John had the same problem. His shoes hurt so bad he tied the strings together and hung 'em around his neck. I'll swear, you could tell where he'd been by following his bloodly tracks in the snow. Then later at the Hindenburg Line, John was gassed and hit by shrapnel in his legs. But he refused to be evacuated for treatment, saying that he'd come this far with his buddies from Lancaster and he wasn't about to turn back now. I don't know how he did it. I know he was in terrible pain, but he refused to quit."

Bill Medford recalls that amid all the terror and confusion of a gas attack, the men usually engaged in a vociferous round of profanity while in a panic to get their gas masks in place. He had grown up with most of the men in his outfit, he says. He knew them, their parents and cousins and everything about them. He remembers one occasion in particular when an old boyhood friend, a young man just arrived at the front, underwent his first experience with a gas attack.

"Someone shouted GAS, and we started cussing and raising hell. We were just as scared as my old friend was, but he had never been under attack before, and he was literally scared to death. Well, he let go a string of profanity that put all the rest of us to shame. We just

Ira Pittman (above) and Charles Caskey were boyhood friends who joined the army together and then served together throughout their enlistments.

Walter E. White (118th Regiment, 30th Infantry Division) was among the first contingent of young men to report for duty on September 1, 1917, and was a combat veteran of both Ypres and the Somme in July and September of 1918. He was discharged in 1919.

John T. Bailey (right) was a medic with the Sanitation Detachment, Battery F, 318th Field Artillery, 81st Division, at Camp Mills, New York in July 1918, just prior to shipping out aboard the Lapland. The 81st arrived at LeHavre, France in August 1918.

stopped what we were doing and stood there staring at him. Yessir, amid all the shot and shell, with clouds of that green gas swirling around us, we all fell perfectly silent.

"I said, 'Now, William, I wouldn't be talking like that if I were you. I know your mother and father, and they certainly wouldn't like it either.'

"Well, later, that struck me as so darned funny. There were a lot of funny things happened in combat."

Many of the humorous anecdotes told by our veterans concern the nighttime misadventures of either themselves or their friends. W.B. Adams, for example, recalls setting up camp one night in a patch of woods following a long march to the Hindenburg Line.

"My buddy—they called him Swede—and I set our tent up right beside a deep shell hole. I finally got in the tent and wrapped up in my blanket, but Swede decided he'd sleep in the shell hole—safer, you know. Well, we had just got to sleep when a big thunder shower came up and the hole started to fill with water. But old Swede didn't move a muscle, just continued to snore away like he was in the Waldorf-Astoria. But then the water got high enough that it ran up Swede's nose. He got strangled, of course, and jumped up out of that hole like his coattails were on fire. He was yelling and all wild eyed, and he ran right through my tent and took off through the woods. The last time I saw him that night he was tearing around through the woods, with my tent flapping around him, hollaring, 'Help me! Help me! Somebody help me!' Of course I got soaking wet too. But still I couldn't help but laugh."

A grinning Coyt Green says, "It was a very bad time at the front, and we'd taken shelter in a little trench about a foot deep with nothing between us and the Germans but open ground. Well, this big chubby boy next to me had been squirming around for hours, complaining that he was dying to urinate. But of course he couldn't. He couldn't do it lying down in that little trench, and if he'd stood up those German machineguns would have cut him in half. So as soon as it got dark, he said, 'Thank God!' and so he hopped out of the trench. Well, he got behind a splintered tree trunk but no sooner had he begun relieving his kidneys than flares began lighting the area and German machinegun bullets began zipping overhead. Well, that boy stopped what he was doing right where he was and started stumbling for the

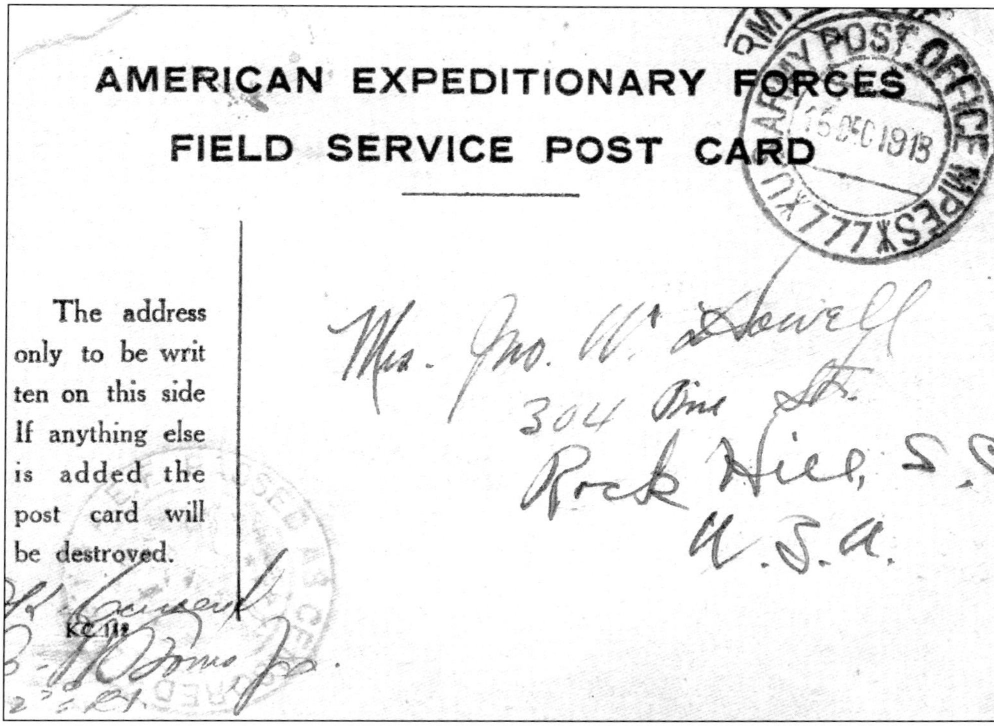

AMERICAN EXPEDITIONARY FORCES

FIELD SERVICE POST CARD

The address only to be written on this side If anything else is added the post card will be destroyed.

Mrs. Jno. W. Howell
304 Pine St.
Rock Hill, S.C.
U.S.A.

William Ford Howell sent this unusual postcard to his mother from France in 1918.

trench, his pants half-way down his legs. He rolled down among us, scared to death, panting like he'd just run a mile, and said, 'If the Lord will spare me this time, I swear I'll never urinate again.' Well, we couldn't help but laugh."

Then came Verdun.

James H. Caskey calls this "the most harrowing experience of my life. The weather was brutally cold, the battlefield a sea of mud, and the men in my outfit were constantly ill with the flu. Land mines were everywhere, and it was here that I got my first glimpse of German tanks."

Heyward F. Hough (6th Infantry Division) remembers the terrain around Verdun as "level and without cover—a bad place to fight. The Germans had thousands of machine guns in place, and they were raised just to the level of a man's knees. When we tried to advance, they mowed us down like wheat, just cut us off at the knees."

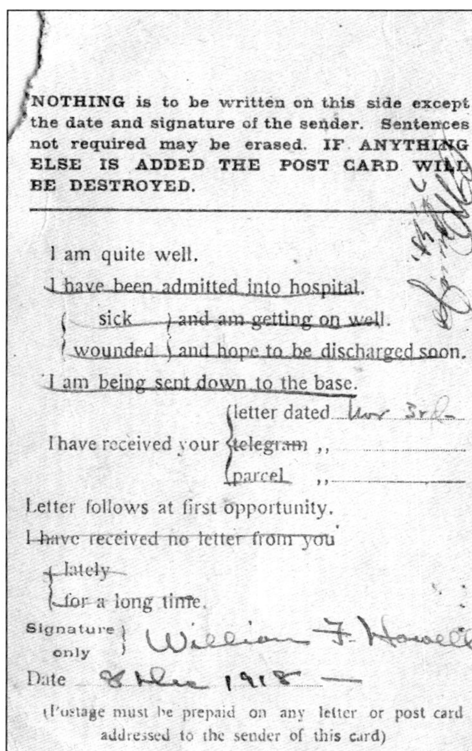

NOTHING is to be written on this side except the date and signature of the sender. Sentences not required may be erased. IF ANYTHING ELSE IS ADDED THE POST CARD WILL BE DESTROYED.

I am quite well.

~~I have been admitted into hospital.~~

~~sick } and am getting on well.~~

~~wounded } and hope to be discharged soon.~~

~~I am being sent down to the base.~~

I have received your letter dated Nov 3rd; ~~telegram~~ ,, ; ~~parcel~~ ,,

Letter follows at first opportunity.

~~I have received no letter from you~~

~~lately~~

~~for a long time.~~

Signature only } William F. Howell

Date 8 Dec 1918 —

(Postage must be prepaid on any letter or post card addressed to the sender of this card)

A medic in the Great War, Francis Laird Schwartz regretted not going to the front. But then he saw how badly he was needed in the army hospitals of America. Following the war, he would become a much beloved Baptist minister, serving the Lancaster area for many years.

A considerably filled out Dickson Barnes Sistare has now been promoted to PFC and is a member of Company G, 156th Depot Brigade. He was discharged in February 1919.

Roland Lattimore shakes his head sadly when reminded of Verdun. "We came in and relieved the French 20th Division who had been fighting the Germans since 1914. I remember us passing them on the road, we moving in and they moving out, and they would yell to us—they called us Sam—they'd yell, 'Hey, Sam, Verdun is the place of the Germans, it is the Germans' place. Not one of you will come out of here alive.' Which is not very reassuring when you're marching up to go into battle. But they were almost right—few of us did come out alive."

It was at Verdun that Lattimore had his most chilling experience of the war. Sleet had been falling all evening and his company had been pinned down for hours in the rubble of a bombed out French village. It was then past midnight and he remembers lying there, his teeth chattering from the cold, sleet stinging his face.

"The cause of all the trouble was a single German machine gun situated behind a stone wall in a little wooded area some 200 yards away. It was zeroed in right on us, firing little short bursts, no matter whether there was anything to shoot at or not. We couldn't figure it out, but many of our men were hit, several killed. Finally, just before daybreak, when we really couldn't stand it any longer, another boy and I volunteered to go out and try to silence the emplacement. So out we went, and we crawled and crawled, until finally we got around behind him and his machine gun. So then I crawled a little closer until I could actually see that German squatting there behind his machine gun. I got to within about five feet of him, then I pointed my .45 at him and yelled HANDS UP or something like that. But he didn't move. Well, I was about to shoot, but then I looked closer and I could see in that early dawn light that his head was nothing but a bloody pulp. He was dead, just sitting there, his finger still frozen to the trigger. I suddenly felt a cold gust of wind, and sure enough that young German soldier rocked back just a little. Rat-tat-tat went the machine gun. Then he rocked forward again and the firing stopped. I reached down and released his finger from the trigger and the firing stopped completely. I've oftern wondered since then how many men that dead German killed that night. But even today when anybody mentions Verdun, that's the kind of thing I still think about."

Frank Fisher remembers the devastating machine gun fire thrown up by the Germans at the Argonne Forest. He remembers crouching in a shallow trench and watching carefully as a German officer came stumbling across No Man's Land waving a white flag and shouting, "Don't shoot! Don't shoot!"

"Of course we held our fire, but then that German officer suddenly leaped down into a shell crater—and that was their signal. Machine gun fire erupted from every direction. It lasted for hours, and when it stopped finally that forest looked as though it had been ripped by a hurricane. Tree limbs were everywhere, and hundreds of our men lay dead. It was a terrible loss for the 97th Infantry."

Another veteran observes that if the machine guns didn't get you, the artillery would. Indeed, by 1918 both sides in the war could fire their artillery pieces with deadly accuracy.

L.O. McManus (21st Heavy Artillery, 5th Infantry Division), who was in charge of a horse-drawn caisson, describes his experiences as a front line artilleryman in terms of frustration and exhaustion.

"There was always mud, mud, mud. We lived in mud, ate in mud, slept in mud. Mud up to our knees. We couldn't walk for it. The horses couldn't walk for it. And if we weren't careful, the big guns would just sink down out of sight in it. So we always had to keep the horses moving, except when we had to stop to station our big guns. Once we did that, then we'd just slog around the best we could and fired. And that's another thing—we never knew what we were firing at. An observer sitting way up in an observation balloon would signal us, you know, and tell us how many rounds to fire, and how much powder to use, and what our elevation

William Ford Howell was in his senior year at Clemson College in April 1917 when his class was told that if they would immediately resign and join the army, Clemson would give them credit for the courses they were taking and mail them their diplomas in June. Howell thus resigned, took basic training at Camp Oglethorpe in Georgia, then went overseas attached to an Army Intelligence group (he was aboard a troopship when his Clemson diploma arrived). He served in France until his discharge in 1919, then, instead of coming home, he returned to England to study horticulture at the University of Bristol. (He returned to Lancaster in 1920 and lived here for another 60 years.)

Henry Grady Burgess (1st Battalion, 1st Provisional Division) remembers that it was just a matter of luck that his life was spared early in his military career.

should be. But he'd never tell us what we were shooting at."

And Vernon Phillips, also a member of the 21st Heavy Artillery, recalls a strange thing about in-coming artillery fire.

"If it was going to land to the left or right of you, you could tell from the sound. But if it was coming straight at you, you'd only hear a whizzing noise. Then you didn't know whether to run forward or backward. You'd just lie flat and pray."

Many of our veterans say they feared their own artillery almost as much as that of the Germans. Bill Medford recalls several occasions when his unit would advance under a barrage set up by American guns.

"The further we advanced, the closer the shells landed around us. And the reason was simple—our artillery was shelling the German front line trenches, which was also our objective. We'd fall down and lie flat for a few seconds, then we'd get up and run forward a little further. Sometimes our shells would fall short, and of course when that happened they would fall right among us. They told us later that five per cent of our men were killed by our own artillery."

Leonard T. Hallman (21st Heavy Artillery, 5th Infantry Division) agrees with Medford. "When the infantry went over the top, they called on us to shell the Germans. We all set our watches, of course, and when the zero hour came, we were supposed to stop firing. But sometimes the infantry advanced too rapidly, and when that happened they ran into their own artillery. Communications were pretty primitive back in those day, and there was just no way our artillery could communicate with our infantry, and that lack of communication resulted in many needless deaths."

But of all his duties, Hallman particularly dreaded having to guard his company's horses and mules at night.

Roland Lattimore (seated) and a friend pose during a lull in the fighting. Lattimore says that life was cheap at the front and he once saw a man lose his life for a can of tomatoes. (This photograph was taken in Paris in 1918.)

"One old mule or another would surely wander off during the night, and when that happened you had to find him and bring him back. It was dark as pitch, of course, and we weren't allowed to use any sort of light. I remember I'd slip up on this old mule, and just as soon as I'd make a grab for his head he'd turn around and I'd grab him by the tail. And he'd squeal like bloody murder, you know, really kick up a row, and the Germans would hear it and think we were launching a general attack. So then they'd start sending up flares and then they'd open up with their machine guns. Then our side

Creighton Threatt fought with Battery F, 120th Field Artillery through some of the bloodiest campaigns of 1918 and was in a Paris hospital when the war ended. (In 1976, he still found it almost impossible to discuss the war.)

would answer with our own machine guns. Before long that old mule would have a full scale battle going on. I was always so glad to see daylight come."

John H. Hinson (135th Field Artillery, 37th Infantry Division) recalls stopping in a little wooded area one quiet, sunny morning to have breakfast. He took a big chunk of hardtack from his pack and had just leaned back against a tree and gotten comfortable when out of no where a German artillery round exploded overhead. It blasted the top out of the tree, and shrapnel knocked Hinson's mess kit from his hand, scattering hardtack and water everywhere. Hinson himself was knocked unconscious, though he wasn't seriously injured. "But still, even today," he says, "I have a tendency to get real nervous when I smell gun powder burning. But that experience just illustrates how easy it was to get killed at the front. The Germans were actually aiming at the front line trenches, and that shell landed back where I was just by accident. But it didn't matter whether it was intentional or accidental. Artillery rounds don't have a conscience, so you were just as dead either way."

Many of our veterans, especially those of the 27th and 30th Infantry Divisions, were involved in the final push against the Hindenburg Line during the summer and fall of 1918.

Oscar Roddy Bell gives the following account of his experiences in this crucial battle:

"We went by train from Perrone, France, to a town called Loutencourt. From there we marched to the front, the backbone of the Hindenburg Line. On September 29, about five a.m., zero hour arrived. We were scared, sure, but in a way you come prepared to do whatever you have to do. You know in advance the dangers you'll face, plus there's this feeling of camaraderie that sustains you in bad moments. I

This citation, signed by President Woodrow Wilson, was presented to Marion Taylor for wounds he received in France.

Charles Catoe (sitting) and his boyhood chum Leonard Thurlow Hallman, members of the 5th Infantry Division (The Red Diamonds), were stationed in Germany as a part of the occupation force following the Armistice.

remember the night before the battle we were all huddled down in our trench and the captain stood there in the darkness and told us we were facing 14 Gereman divisions and that we'd be overwhelmed if our attack failed.

"So for the next two days we fought like wild men. My regiment captured over 5,000 German prisoners. God knows how many thousands we killed. Then we were relieved and sent back to Perrone for a rest. But as luck would have it, the Germans counterattacked that night and we were sent back to the front. I remember we were then positioned in an area that was totally open, no protection anywhere. It was then that I saw for the first time British cavalry go into action. They came out of a little wooded area off to our right, and they were standing in their stirrups, leaning forward against the wind, and carrying long lances. Then the Germans opened up with their machine guns, firing at point blank range, right into the midst of them. Hundreds of those Britishers were swept from their saddles, just like wheat being cut down. It was a real slaughter.

"Then a big shell exploded near me and I was knocked unconscious and severely gassed. I lay there for some ten hours before anyone could get out to move me to an aid station. I can remember lying there and an old friend came up. He stood there looking down at me and said, 'Poor old Sergeant Bell. He ain't gonna make it.'

"The bottom of our trench was covered in blood, and I can remember lying there that night watching the glitter of stars reflecting in the pools of blood."

Later, after recovering from his wounds, Bell would return to the front, to an area of the Hindenburg Line known as the St. Quinton Canal. The battle was over by then, and Bell and his old friend, J.P. Richards, decided to explore the canal.

Bell recalls a grim experience: "We entered the canal dam by an underground entrance and walked down a long, winding stairway that led to a large concrete room deep beneath the earth. We looked around in surprise, for the room was empty except for three huge iron pots, about thirty feet in diameter, which sat upon big grates filled with dead coals. Those pots were filled with water, which led J.P. and me to suppose that we'd discovered a German kitchen. I remember we got us a big box and climbed up on it and peered down into one of those big pots of murky water, thinking maybe we'd found us some delicious soup. But then we saw what it was, and we gasped and jumped back in revulsion. The pots were filled with the bodies of dead German soldiers. We found out later that they were being boiled down for their fat, an essential ingredient in making gun powder.

"Well, J.P. and I decided to get out of there. We were backing up rather quickly towards the stairway when a body suddenly swirled upright in one of those pots. He was a blond, crew-cut German lad. And I still remember, I can still see that boy when I close my eyes, he had the bluest eyes I've ever seen."

As for J.P. Richards, he would soon be commissioned a second lieutenant and given command of a Stokes Trench Battery. Of the 48 men under his command, only 13 would survive the war.

Bill Medford also has dark memories of the Hindenburg Line and the St. Quinton Canal. He recalls that many of his friends were killed there. So many, in fact, that the army could not pause long enough in its rapid advance against the retreating Germans to give them a Christian burial.

"The Old Hickory Division was the first to reach the Hindenburg Line, and then we rested at the St. Quinton Canal just long enough to give our supply line time to catch up with us. I can remember so many of the men from my unit who were killed there. Their bodies were rolled up in burlap, then they were buried one atop the other in two long, shallow trenches, 75 in one trench, 74 in the other. Just stacked them up like a deck of cards. Then we were on the move again. It made me feel bad that we couldn't at least give them a decent burial. I don't know whatever happened to their remains.

Leonard Thurlow Hallman (seated left) and James Cauthen (seated right), friends since childhood, were both member of the 21st Heavy Artillery, 5th Infantry Division (The Red Diamonds). Cauthen was stricken with the flu and spent much of the war in the hospital, but Hallman saw action in France throughout 1918.

That was half a century ago now. I guess they're still there. I always wondered what would happen if those poor boys' parents ever went there trying to find their son's grave."

For John H. Hinson the Hindenburg Line was a nightmare which he will never forget, though he wishes he could.

"I especially remember approaching the Hindenburg Line our first day at the front. I remember advancing through this terribly humid swamp, which had been the scene of a terrible battle some weeks before. I could see nothing before me but mud, water, fog and shattered

Fred Horton (bottom right, with his arm around a friend) has written on this card: "A bunch of Rockies with their guns." By now, he was a sergeant serving with Company H, 6th Infantry Division. He was severly wounded at the Somme in October 1918.

tree stumps. And everywhere there lay the decaying corpses of men killed in a great battle. I remember when we first spotted those corpses and realized where we were. We got so quiet that you could've heard a pin drop.

"That swamp seemed to go on forever and ever, and the oder of decaying bodies hung over everything like a big wet blanket. There were bodies under every bush, behind every tree, floating in the shallow pools of water, some American and British, some German. Many of them were submerged in the mud, and they were so thick together that we walked through that swamp and hardly got our feet wet."

Indeed, for many, such as J.A. Weston and Creighton M. Threatt, the experiences of war were so devastating that they still refuse to discuss it.

Yet our veterans did not spend all their time on the front lines. Somehow, many found time for recreation in France.

Ben C. Hough, for example, found time to romance a beautiful French girl. He tells the following poignant story:

"She was beautiful. That, really, is all you have to know. But I was off on a weekend pass, and I met her on a train somewhere between Paris and Marseille. She was sitting on the seat across from me, and I wanted so badly to say hello, but I spoke little French and she spoke almost no English. But we managed to communicate somehow, and she told me she was from Issoudun. We felt something for each other immediately, and later she studied English, at least enough that we could write to one another. From then on, we would meet on the weekends, and we formed a wonderful relationship. Just before I left France to return to America she had a French artist in Issoudun paint her picture for me. Of course I promised I would return after the war and we would be married. But you know how that goes. So I came back home and sure enough I became interested in someone else.

"It was a long time before I went back, but then in 1946, just after World War II ended, I returned to Issoudun to find her. But she wasn't there. The Second World War had just ended and Issoudun had been ravaged. Armies had passed through and almost nothing was left standing. There was just ruin everywhere. So I went to see the Chief of Police. He said, 'Mr. Hough, we have had another war since you were here. General Patton's Third Army blew Issoudun away. This is only a ghost you're looking at now.'

"Well, to make a long story short, I never saw her again. But even today I still think of her."

Roland Lattimore remembers making friends with an elderly French couple who lived near where his company was encamped. He became very fond of this couple, though there were some problems in communications.

"I had a French dictionary, but we still had trouble communicating. But they kept two chickens there in the backyard and in the house, and I thought if I talked to them they might sell me some eggs. Well, I got out my little dictionary and I pointed to the hens and I said, 'Oeufs.' Then I said, 'Comme sa,' speaking to the old woman. Then I said, 'Oeufs' again and held up four fingers. So she went around back of her house and brought me four eggs. I didn't know how to count French money either, so I just reached in my pocket and took out my change and held it out to her. She took what she wanted and gave me the rest back. So I went back to camp and ate all four of those eggs at one time."

John H. Caskey says that the war changed his entire outlook on life. "Things that were unimportant to me before the war, such as religion, character, compassion, became uppermost in my mind once I'd been in battle."

W.B. Adams also supplemented his meager army rations with goods purchased from French civilians. And, like Lattimore, he paid for his goods by simply holding out all his money and letting the seller take whatever was owed. He recalls an old French couple who gave him a glass of milk one day.

"It was so good, and it'd been so long since I'd had any good milk, I went ahead and bought a whole quart of milk and drank it with my supper—that was

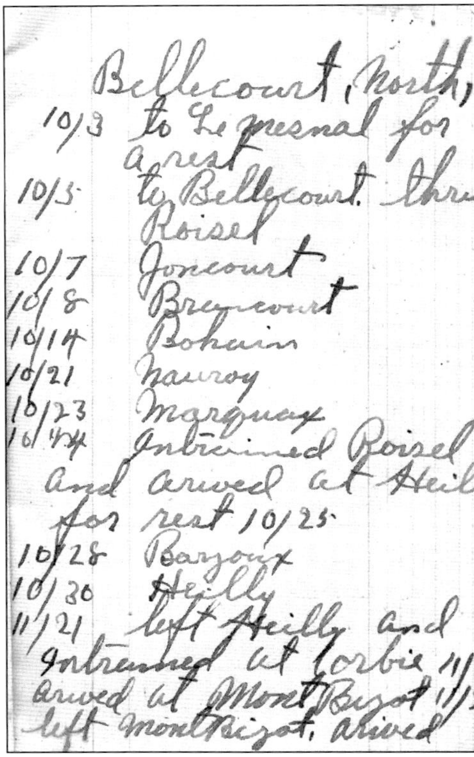
Bellecourt, North,
10/3 to Le Fresnal for a rest
10/5 to Bellecourt thru Roisel
10/7 Joncourt
10/8 Brancourt
10/14 Bohain
10/21 Mauroy
10/23 Marquay
10/24 Intrained Roisel and arrived at Heilly for rest 10/25
10/28 Baryoux
10/30 Heilly
11/21 left Heilly and intrained at Corbie 11/2
arrived at Mont Bizot 11/2
left Mont Bizot, arrived

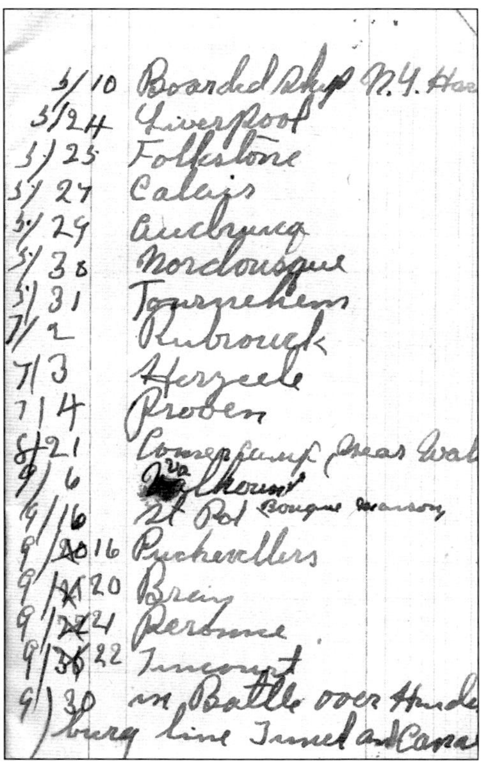
5/10 Boarded Ship N.Y. Har
5/24 Liverpool
5/25 Folkestone
5/27 Calais
5/29 Audruicq
5/30 Nordausque
5/31 Tournehem
7/2 Rubrouck
7/3 Herzeele
7/4 Proven
8/21 Camp near Wat
9/6 Walkourt
9/16 St Pol Bougue Maison
9/16 Puchevillers
9/20 Brain
9/21 Peronne
9/22 Tincourt
9/30 in Battle over Hindenburg line Tunnel and Cana

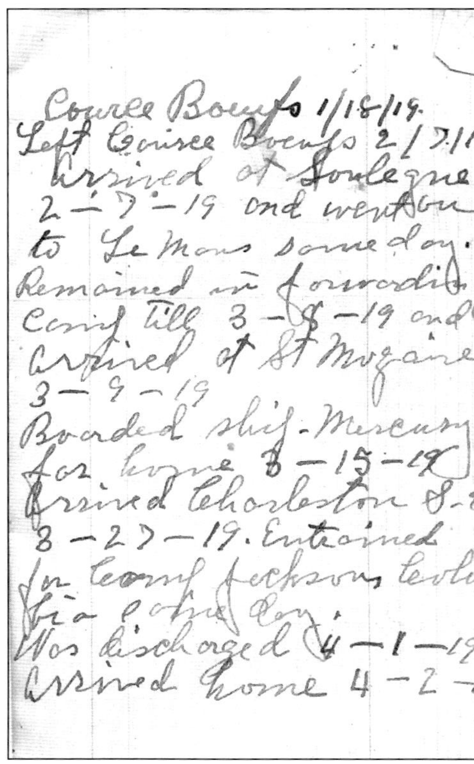
Conree Boeufs 1/18/19.
Left Conree Boeufs 2/7/19
Arrived at Boulogne 2-7-19 and went on to Le Mans same day.
Remained in forwarding camp till 3-8-19 and arrived at St Nazaire 3-9-19
Boarded ship Mercury for home 3-15-19
Arrived Charleston S.C. 3-27-19. Entrained for Camp Jackson Columbia same day.
Was discharged 4-1-19
Arrived home 4-2-

"All the News That's Fit to Print."

The New York Times.

THE WEATHER

VOL. LXVIII...NO. 22,206. NEW YORK, MONDAY, NOVEMBER 11, 1918. TWENTY-FOUR PAGES. TWO CENTS

ARMISTICE SIGNED, END OF THE WAR! BERLIN SEIZED BY REVOLUTIONISTS NEW CHANCELLOR BEGS FOR ORDE OUSTED KAISER FLEES TO HOLLAN

SON FLEES WITH EX-KAISER

Hindenburg Also Believed to be Among Those in His Party.

ALL ARE HEAVILY ARMED

Automobiles Bristle with Rifles as Fugitives Arrive at Dutch Frontier.

ON THEIR WAY TO DE STEEG

Belgians Yell to Them, "Are You On Your Way to Paris?"

Kaiser Fought Hindenburg's Call for Abdication; Failed to Get Army's Support in Keeping Throne

By GEORGE RENWICK.

BERLIN TROOPS JOIN REVOLT

Reds Shell Building in Which Officers Vainly Resist.

THRONGS DEMAND REPUBLIC

Revolutionary Flag on Royal Palace — Crown Prince's Palace Also Seized.

GENERAL STRIKE IS BEGUN

Burgomaster and Police Submit—War Office Now Under Socialist Control.

Socialist Chancellor Appeals to All Germans To Help Him Save Fatherland from Anarchy

WAR ENDS AT 6 O'CLOCK THIS

The State Department in Wa Made the Announcement 2:45 o'Clock.

ARMISTICE WAS SIGNED IN FRANCE AT

Terms Include Withdrawal from Alsace Disarming and Demobilization of Ar Navy, and Occupation of Strat Naval and Military Points.

GERMAN DYNASTIES BEING WIPED OUT

King of Wuerttemberg Abdicates — Sovereign of Saxony to Follow Suit.

PRINCES MAY BE EXILED

Socialists Are Demanding That Every Sovereign in the Empire Shall be Dethroned.

MORE WARSHIPS JOIN THE REDS

Four Dreadnoughts in Kiel Harbor for Espouse the Revolutionary Cause.

GUARDSHIPS ALSO GO OVER

Those Protecting Mines in the Great Belt and the Baltic Abandon Their Posts.

By The Associated Press.

WASHINGTON, Monday, Nov. 1 M.—The armistice between Germany, c hand, and the allied Governments United States, on the other, has been s

The State Department announce o'clock this morning that Germa signed.

The department's announcement said: "The armistice has been signe

The world war will end this morn o'clock, Washington time, 11 o'clock Pa

The armistice was signed by the representatives at midnight.

This announcement was made by t Department at 2:50 o'clock this mornir

The announcement was made verb an officila of the State Department in th

"The armistice has been signed. signed at 5 o'clock A. M., Paris time, [mi New York time,] and hostilities will cea o'clock this morning, Paris time, [6 o'clo York time.]

The terms of the armistice, it w nounced, will not be made public unti

Headlines from the New York Times, *November 11, 1918.*

on Monday. On Tuesday I went back and bought some more. On the third day I went back and bought another quart. I thought it was the best and richest cow's milk I'd ever tasted. Well, on Thursday I went back again. I went in their cottage, made milking signs with my hands, gave the old woman my money, then waited while she went out back to milk her cow. A few minutes later she came back with the milk and I took a big swig of it. So then I walked outside feeling very happy, and just happened to walk around back to take

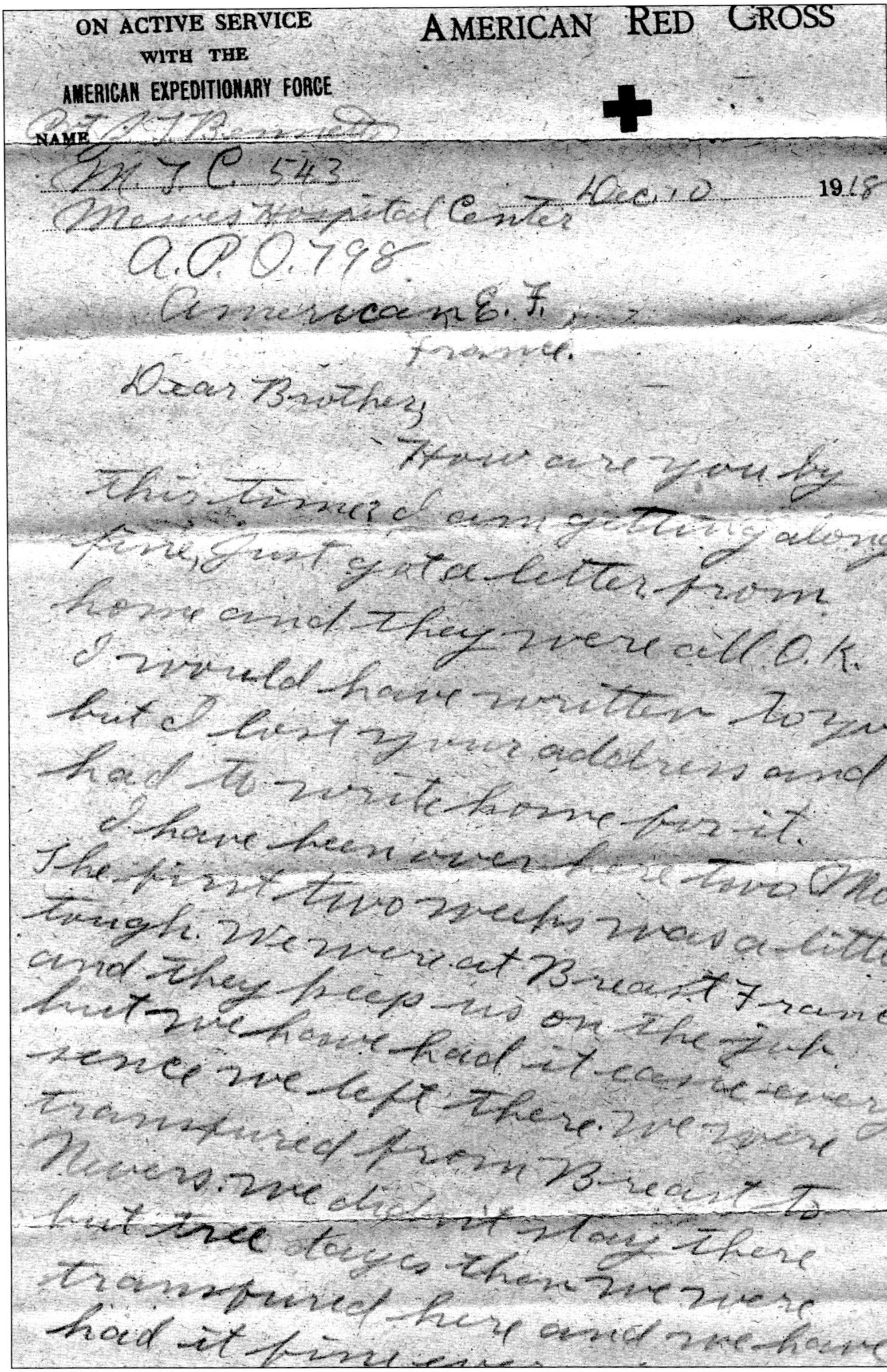

ON ACTIVE SERVICE
WITH THE
AMERICAN EXPEDITIONARY FORCE

AMERICAN RED CROSS

NAME Pvt. J. T. Bennett

M. T. C. 543

Mesves Hospital Center

Dec. 10 1918

A.P.O. 798

American E. F.

France.

Dear Brother

How are you by this time. I am getting along fine. Just got a letter from home and they were all O.K. I would have written to you but I lost your address and had to write home for it.

I have been over here two Mo. The first two weeks was a little tough. We were at Breast France and they keep us on the jump but we have had it easy ever since we left there. We were transfured from Breast to Nevers. we didn't stay there but tree days then we were transfured here and we have had it fine ever

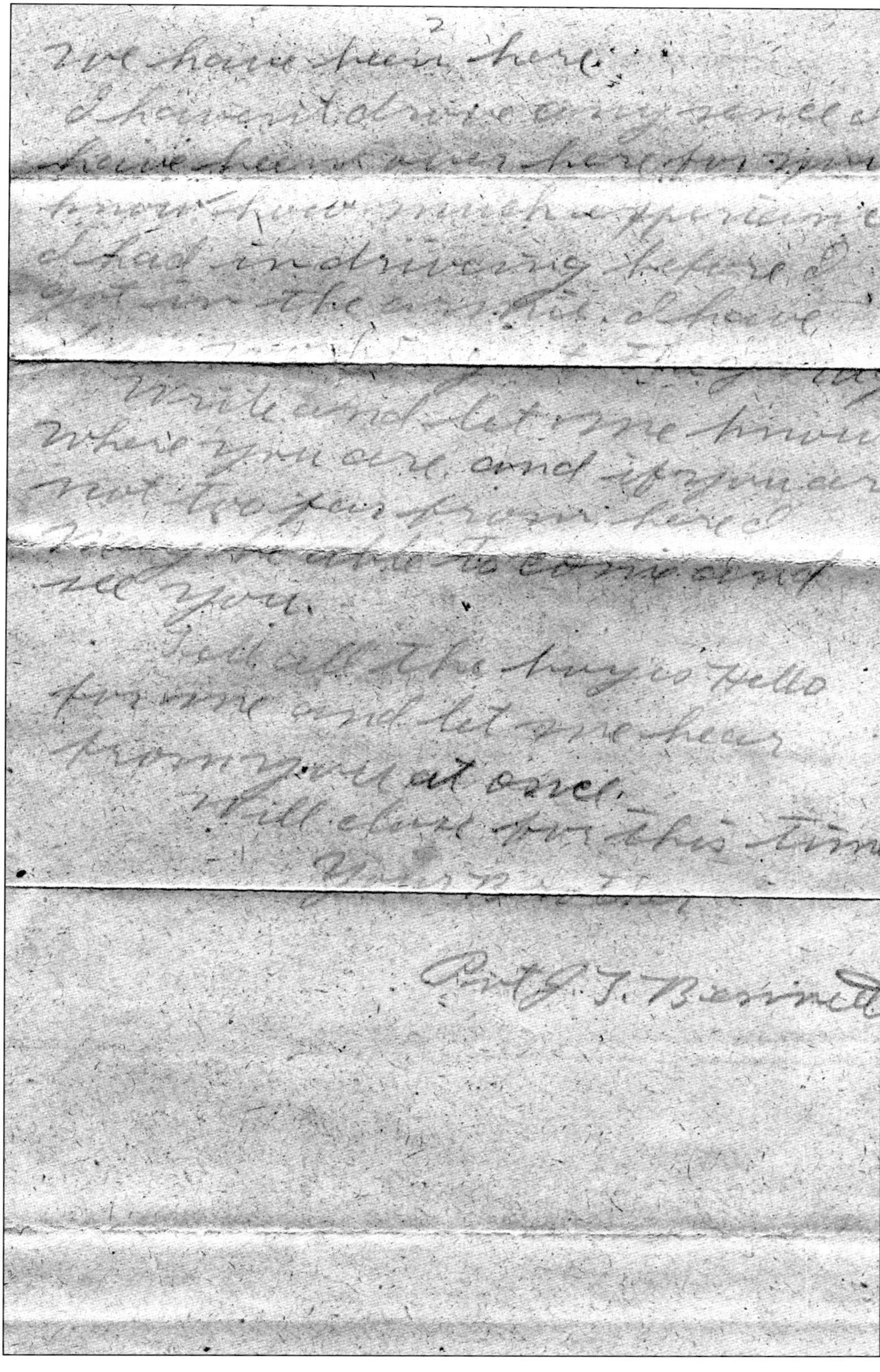

we have been here.

I haven't drove any since I have been over here for you know how much experience I had in driving before I got in the service. I have

Write and let me know where you are, and if you are not too far from here I may be able to come and see you.

Tell all the boys hello for me and let me hear from you at once.

Will close for this time

Yours

Pvt J. T. Bennett

Franklyn Pierce Bell (seated) was inducted in September 1917, and was assigned to Company E, 118th Regiment, 30th Infantry Division. He received wounds and suffered from shell shock during the Battle of the Argonne Forest in October 1918. At war's end, he received a Presidential Citation for bravery from Woodrow Wilson.

John B. Faulkenberry (118th Regiment, 30th Infantry Division) saw action at the Hindenburg Line. He was gassed and hit with shrapnel in his leg, but refused treatment, saying that he wanted to press onward with his friends from Lancaster.

a look at that wonderful cow. Well, there was that old woman, and she was milking the most broken down, mangiest looking old goat you've ever seen. I gave that milk to the first man I came across. Told him I was just tired of milk."

How Ya Gonna Keep 'Em Down on the Farm After They've Seen Paree?

On November 11, 1918, the Germans surrendered, the Armistice was announced, and thus ended of one of the most horrible wars in history. Today, almost 60 years following the end of that war, veterans of all nationalities still have vivid memories of the great celebrations that erupted throughout the Western World.

For Vance Bailey the Armistice could not have come at a better time. He remembers that he was in Newport News, Virginia, and had just boarded a Kennedy Cattle Boat for France when the news arrived that the fighting was all over. He still smiles at the memory.

"Everyone at the docks began shouting and throwing their caps in the air. There were a lot of nurses and Red Cross ladies standing there waiting to see us off, and I lifted one up in my arms, a truly beautiful nurse, and pretended that I was going to take her to France with us. Well, she started kissing me until I got downright embarrassed and had to put her down and tell her that I was just joking. I really believe she would have gone with us. But everyone was so happy that all the killing and maiming was over. Well, the next day they unloaded us off the boat again and some of us were sent to these stables to wash the horses and clean up after them. But we were so happy we spent the day singing to the horses."

For Bill Medford the Armistice meant a night on the town in a French village with some friends, then a wonderful seven-day leave in London.

Sim Harrison Plyler (3rd Army) reached France at the war's end and then was stationed in Koblintz, Germany, following the war. His mother predicted that he'd not live to see his wife and daughter again, but despite her dire predictions, Plyler returned home and fathered seven more children.

Ira L. Vernon Phillips (21st Heavy Artillery, 5th Infantry "The Red Diamond" Division) fought through France, then would become a part of the occupation force in Germany following the war.

Vernon Phillips (marked with an X) and his gun crew of the 21st Heavy Artillery paused for this photograph.

Gen. John Pershing reviews the 5th Infantry in Luxemburg at war's end. (Someone has written in pen "My Daddy's picture" over the likeness of Vernon Phillips in the above photograph.)

"That night in that French village we drank as much champagne and wine as we could hold. This was way back in a French village that had been untouched by the war, and we were in a brightly lit beer garden, and we were all running around, you know, trying to borrow money from each other to buy more wine with and just having a high old time. Then the next morning seven of us took off for London. What a free, wonderful, hilarious week that was after a year in the trenches. I have never seen as many people as there were jammed into one place as there were in Piccadilly Square the night of November 12th. Everyone was drunk with excitement, and if you got caught in a crowd going in this direction, you went in this direction, or in that direction. I saw a horse-drawn hack caught up in that crowd and literally crushed.

"Believe it or not, soldiers were at a premium in England at that time, and my friend Charlie and I met a couple of real nice girls there. Not nobility or anything, but real nice girls by the name of Doris and Alice Silver. We'd take

Walter S. Watson (right) of the 162nd Transport Guard Regiment was stationed in St. Florentine, France. He saw heavy action in 1918 and returned to Elgin in 1919 to operate Watson's Cotton Gin.

A LIVE PAPER IN A LIVE TOWN

THE LANCASTER NEWS

COTT 28

68TH YEAR. NO. 7. SEMI-WEEKLY. LANCASTER, S. C., TUESDAY, NOVEMBER 12, 1918. SUBSCRIPTION $2.00

EVERYTHING AMERICA FOUGHT F
HAS NOW BEEN FULLY ACCOMPLISH

PRESIDENT WILSON ANNOUNCES SIGNING OF ARMISTICE AND TERMS ACCEPTED BY THE GERMAN GOVERNMENT WHICH ENDS WAR

PRESIDENT APPEARS BEFORE CONGRESS IN JOINT SESSION

Everything for Which This Country Fought Overseas Is Attained.

GERMANY ACCEPTS THE MOST DRASTIC TERMS

Measures Taken By Allied Governments Make it Impossible for Germany to Again Take Up Arms Against the Entente Nations.

Washington, Nov. 11.—Signing of the armistice with Germany was proclaimed today by President Wilson, who also announced its terms at a joint session of congress.

THE "WAR LORD" OF EUROPE STEPS OUT

Abdication of Kaiser and Renunciation of Trone By Crown Prince.

REGENCY TO BE SET UP

All Heads of Governments of Central Powers at Beginning of War Have Died or Lost Their Thrones.

William Hohenzollern, German emperor and king of Prussia, has decided to renounce the throne.

This declaration is made in a decree issued at Berlin by the German imperial chancellor, Prince Maximilian, of Baden. The German crown prince will also renounce the throne, and a regency will be set up.

Prince Maxmilian will remain in office until matters connected with

MUST STAND BY THE VICTORIOUS TROOPS

Until Last Brave Boy is Home Again There Must Be No Slackening.

QUOTA MUST BE RAISED

Encouraging Reports Received at State Headquarters in Columbia Promising Support in War Work Campaign.

Columbia, S. C., Nov. 11.—Will South Carolina do her full duty by the victorious American troops in Europe, guaranteeing to them all possible cheer and comfort until the last brave boy is home again?

This question is being answered vigorously in the affirmative at the state headquarters of the United Wark Work campaign, where optimistic telegrams and promises of

GREATER NEED NOW THAN EVER BEFORE

Demobilization Period Frought With Many Dangers for Boys Abroad.

NEED OVERSUBSCRIPTION

United War Work Campaign Goes Forward and More Than Quota for Each State is Necessary.

Colonel Leroy Springs, chairman for Lancaster county of the United War Work campaign, has received the following telegram:

"Following telegram received from Dr. Mott with request to relay same to you:

"United conclusion of the United War Work campaign committee is that no matter how near or how distant permanent peace may be, the long period of demobilization and the period which will precede demobilization will present greater need than ever for the services of the seven cooperative organizations and therefore that the requested oversubscription of fifty per cent is most necessary. Our advisors in the army and navy concur in this judgment. I

ROBERT W. NEAL IS KILLED IN ACTION

A telegram was received by relatives here this morning announcing that Robert W. Neal, of Lancaster, R. F. D. 1, was killed in action September 29. He was a son of Mrs. Mary L. Neal, and a brother of Miss Jennie Neal and Mrs. Dora Hilliard, of this city.

TWO LANCASTER BOYS DIED AT CANTON, OHIO

Remains of Keaver Sowell and George Williams Brought Here Saturday for Burial.

The remains of Keaver Sowell and George Williams reached Lancaster from Canton, Ohio, Saturday morning and were interred at Douglas in the same grave, Rev. T. A. Dabney conducting the funeral services. The two boys had been working in Canton for some time, having left here together, worked together and died same day. Keaver Sowell was the son of R. B. Sowell, of the Jones Cross Roads section, and George Williams was the son of W. J. Williams, of the same community.

Both the boys were about the same age, 18, and had many friends in the community where they were raised. The funeral and burial was attended by a large crowd of sympathetic friends and relatives.

GYPSY SMIT TO A GREA

Weather Made practicable House W

A REMARKAB

Besides Bringin Strong Poin Delightfully With Vivid P

The most re heard in this city Smith in the oper ing at eleven o'cl bringing home m he delightfully en dience with a vi dier life in the peared here in t united war work began yesterday overfilled the op two or three tim scheduled to spe it was so cold th was afraid to a crowd consequent appointed when only about one the building. T marched down i it was decided

them out to dinner, then sit on a park bench afterwards and talk—and do a little courting on the side, of course. We did get picked up by a damned second lieutenant once for not saluting, but other than that, the week of November 12 to 19 was one I'll never forget.

"Oh, and I'll mention this too. While we were there Charlie decided he wanted to buy a new pair of boots. So we were trying to act as adult as possible, you know, and we went into this very fashionable bootery, and Charlie picked out the pair of boots he wanted, then he asked this very sophisticated English clerk how much he owed him. The clerk sort of looked down his nose at us, and said, 'Three guineas.' Well, Charlie and I, being the two young country boys we were, we just looked at each other. Where we came from a guinea was a little bitty knee-high thing that laid eggs and ran out in front of wagons. We figured the clerk was pulling our leg, so we just smiled, thanked him and left."

H.M. Robinson says that years after the Armistice he heard the song *When The Lights Go On Again All Over The World*, and the lyrics brought back so vividly his experiences the night the Great War ended.

"After years of darkness, the soldiers at the front were allowed to build fires again. I remember that evening I strolled back to a high hill just to the rear of our trenches and looked out over miles of flat battle grounds. Only now the battles had stopped and there

was the most beautiful silence I've ever heard. And as far as I could see, the plains were covered with small groups of men, both American and German, sitting around little fires, just relaxing, enjoying being alive. The landscape was dotted with those little fires and men sitting around thanking God to be alive. Believe me, it was a wonderful moment. I stood there and began to weep."

Roland Lattimore remembers that he was crouched down in a deep trench sweating out an intense German artillery barrage when his company commander announced that the firing would cease at exactly 11 a.m. "But stay where you are," admonished the captain. "If you start celebrating too soon, the Germans might overrun our position." So they waited, says Lattimore, the barrage growing in intesity as the morning progressed. Finally, with the shells still crashing down all around them, their chaplain raised up just long enough to say, "Men, after all we've been through during the past year, I don't think it would hurt a thing if we just sort of got up and started moving quietly to the rear, do you?"

"That was just the signal we'd all been waiting for," laughs Lattimore. "We all got up and ran like hell."

E.C. Erickson still has vivid memories of the day the war ended, but he doesn't recall that the men spent any time in celebration. In fact, he's sure of it.

"Well, we might've taken a little drink now and then," he grins.

And Lee Skipper, the aviator, recalls that his flight wing took taxis into Tours and spent the evening trying to drink all the champagne in town.

Robert Rowell (156th Depot Brigade, 3rd Army) , a cousin of Sim Plyler, was likewise stationed in Koblintz following the war.

Ben Hough says the day of the Armistice left no time for celebration. Instead, he was assigned to a clean up crew and sent to the front lines, the scene of a recent battle.

"We picked up arms, legs, heads, bodies, whatever, and threw them into big trucks. Then we had to unload them into deep holes, maybe two or three hundred body parts to a hole. Then we had to cover them up. The oder was terrible and we had to tie handkerchiefs around our faces in order not to gag. For me, it was the worst day of the war."

Coming Home

The firing stopped at exactly 11 a.m., of the 11th day of the 11th month, 1918. And soon the armies would be returning to America, to even wilder celebrations and ticker-tape parades down Fifth Avenue in New York. The experiences of W.B. Adams at this time, though perhaps not typical, are at least interesting and epitomize the dreams of all returning servicemen.

"We were the first soldiers back," he says, "and we stayed in New York for six weeks. There were hundreds of chorus girls and show girls who'd come out to the camp to entertain us. Well, one night, bless gosh, one of those ladies invited me home to have supper with her, and I, like a crazy gump, I accepted. I was married but I didn't care, you know? I mean, I wasn't up to anything or anything. I told her that I was from Lancaster and all about myself, and she, to my amazement, later sent a write up about me to the editor of Lancaster's newspaper. Of course I was married and it kind of worried me. But my wife didn't read it." Adams shakes his head in frustration. "But you might know her sister-in-law did read it and she sent it to my wife. But there was no harm in it. I mean I wasn't up to anything or anything. You know?"

The shooting war was over, yes, but there existed at this time another enemy which was claiming victims by the millions—the flu. It was called the Spanish flu, but where it originated, or how it originated, no one seems to know, though it would claim some 25,000,000 victims throughout the Western World in 1918. The Rev. Francis L. Schwartz says that it began in Europe, in the filty, germ-ridden trenches of France and Belgium, and was inadvertantly introduced to the United States by returning wounded soldiers.

Leonard Thurlow Hallman enjoyed shipboard life so much as a soldier that he decided to serve a hitch in the navy once his tour with the army ended. He served aboard an oil tanker, the U.S.S. Trinity.

"If you were hit by a bullet you had a chance," he says, "but the flu was fatal."

And Frank Fisher says, "So many were dying of the flu in France that we ran out of coffins to bury them. We would take their bodies out and pile them up in big trucks. Then we'd bury them in trenches ten feet deep, their bodies stacked one atop the other."

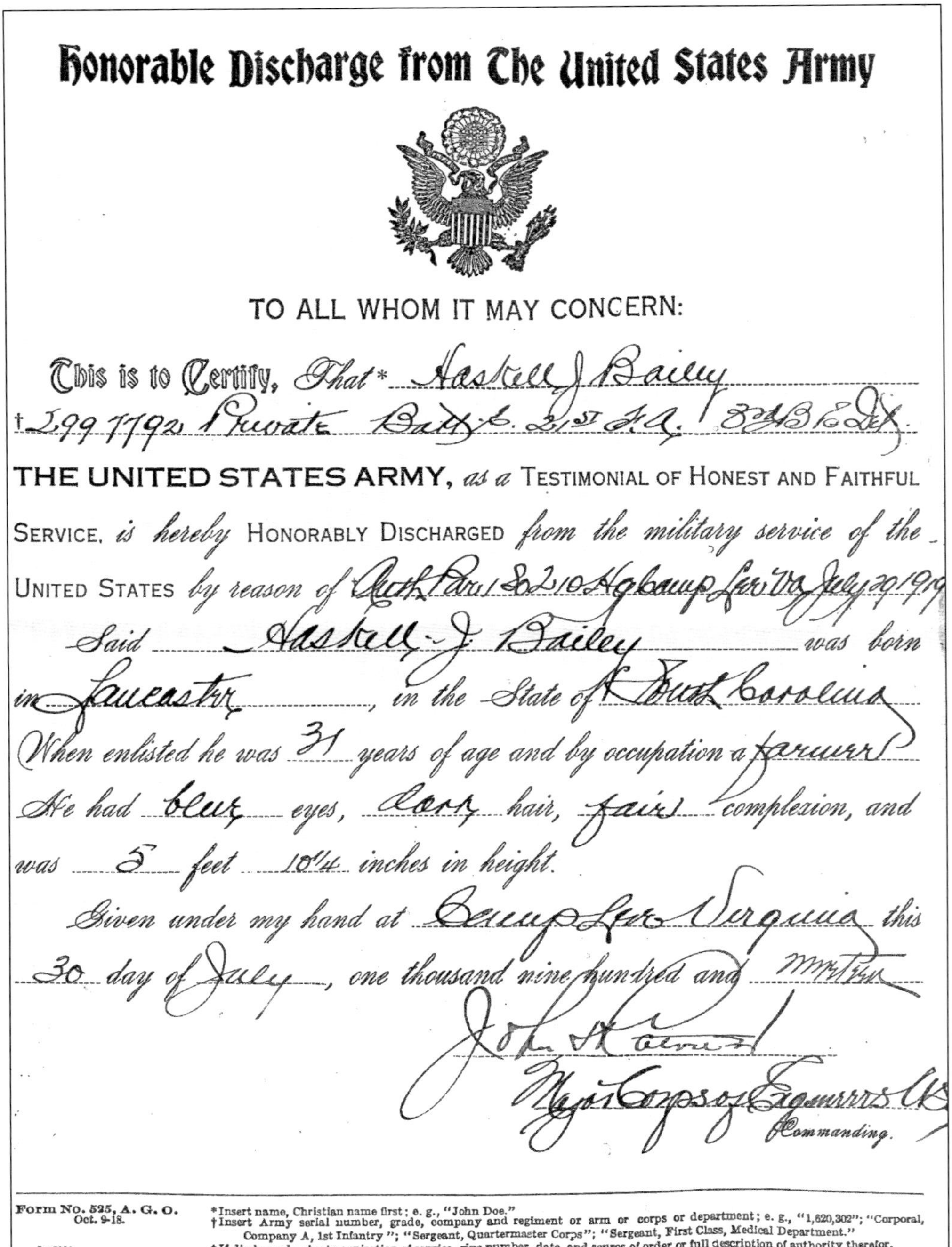

Honorable Discharge from The United States Army

TO ALL WHOM IT MAY CONCERN:

This is to Certify, That* Haskell J Bailey

†2997792 Private Batty C. 21st F.A. 83rd B.F. Det

THE UNITED STATES ARMY, *as a* TESTIMONIAL OF HONEST AND FAITHFUL SERVICE, *is hereby* HONORABLY DISCHARGED *from the military service of the* UNITED STATES *by reason of*‡ Auth Par 1 S.O. 210 Hq Camp Lee Va July 29 1919

Said Haskell J Bailey *was born in* Lancaster, *in the State of* South Carolina

When enlisted he was 31 *years of age and by occupation a* farmer

He had blue *eyes,* dark *hair,* fair *complexion, and was* 5 *feet* 10¼ *inches in height.*

Given under my hand at Camp Lee Virginia *this* 30 *day of* July, *one thousand nine hundred and* nineteen

John H. [illegible]
Major Corps of Engineers U.S.A.
Commanding.

Form No. 525, A. G. O. Oct. 9-18.

*Insert name, Christian name first; e. g., "John Doe."
†Insert Army serial number, grade, company and regiment or arm or corps or department; e. g., "1,620,302"; "Corporal, Company A, 1st Infantry"; "Sergeant, Quartermaster Corps"; "Sergeant, First Class, Medical Department."
‡If discharged prior to expiration of service, give number, date, and source of order or full description of authority therefor.

3—3164

"And no one was immune to the flu," says E.C. Erickson, "not even those at sea serving aboard our ships. I was aboard the *Nevada Land* in 1918, and came down with it and was unconscious for two weeks. But one of our pharmacist mates kept me alive on a diet of Scotch and raw eggs." Erickson remembers that once the *Nevada Land* reached New York they were not allowed to enter the harbor until after they'd returned to open waters and buried their dead

OFFICE OF THE ADJUTANT GENERAL

DIVISION OF WAR RECORDS

COLUMBIA, S. C., Mch 2 1921

THIS is to certify that the records of this office show the service of Thomas V. Bailey

IN THE WORLD WAR TO BE AS FOLLOWS:-

Army serial number: 2,997,653 ~~RA~~ ~~NG~~ ~~ERC~~ NA. White - ~~Colored~~

Residence at entry into service: Lancaster, S.C. RFD #3

~~Enlisted or~~ Inducted at: Lanwaster, S.C. June 23/18

Place of birth: Lancaster, S.C.

Age or date of birth: Dec.1/93

Organization served in, with dates: 14 Co 156 Dep Brig June 29/18; Btry B 8 Regt FARD Camp Jackson, S.C. to disch.

Grades, with date of appointment: Pvt.

Engagements:

Served overseas from: - - - - - - to

Wounded in action: Killed in action:

Died of wounds received in action:

Died of:

Person notified of death:

Honorably discharged: Dec.9/18 19 Cause: On demobilization

Reported 0 per cent. disabled on date of discharge.

Remarks:

Jas. C. Dozier

THE ADJUTANT GENERAL

at sea. "I'll never forget, there were 480 corpses aboard ship that day and we had to drop them all over the side. Then we spread oil all over the sea around us and set it on fire. We had to sit in a circle of fire for 24 hours before they'd let us enter the harbor."

Howard K. Williamson, like thousands of other American soldiers, came down with the flu almost immediately following the end of the war and then spent months in a French hospital, hovering between life and death. Within weeks, his flu turned into pneumonia

DO NOT FEAR INFLUENZA!

Learn How to Avoid It, How to Care for Those Who Have It, What to Do if You Get It

If you feel a sudden chill, followed by muscular pain, headache, backache, unusual tiredness and fever, go to bed at once.

See that there is enough bed clothing to keep you warm and make you sweat.

See that you get plenty of fresh air.

Take medicine to open the bowels freely.

Take some nourishing food, such as milk, egg-and-milk or broth, every four hours.

Stay in bed until a physician tells you it is safe to get up.

Allow no one else to sleep in the same room.

Protect others by sneezing or coughing into handkerchiefs or cloths, which should be boiled or burned.

Insist that whoever gives you water or food or enters the sick room for any other purpose shall wear a gauze mask, which may be obtained at home of four or six folds of gauze and which should cover the nose and mouth and be tied behind the head.

Remember that these masks must be kept clean, must be put on outside the sick room, must not be handled after they are tied on and must be boiled thirty minutes and thoroughly dried every time they are taken off.

The city of Lancaster was hit hard by the flu epidemic during the fall and winter of 1918. This advice to readers appeared in the Lancaster News *on November 1, 1918.*

What to Do Until the Doctor Comes

To Householders:

Keep out of the sick room unless attendance is necessary.

Do not handle articles coming from the sick room until they are boiled.

Allow no visitors, and do not go visiting.

Call a doctor for all inmates who show signs of beginning sickness.

The usual symptoms are: Inflamed and watery eyes, discharging nose, backache, headache, muscular pain and fever.

Keep away from crowded places, such as movies and theaters.

See to it that your children are kept warm and dry, both night and day.

Have sufficient fire in your home to disperse the dampness.

Open your windows at night. If cool weather prevails, add extra bed clothing.

Walk to work if possible.

Avoid the person who coughs or sneezes.

Wash your hands before eating.

To Workers:

Make full use of all available sunshine.

Do not use a common towel. It spreads disease.

Should you cough or sneeze, cover nose and mouth with a handkerchief.

Keep out of crowded places. Walk in the open air rather than go to crowded places of amusement.

Sleep is necessary for well-being—get nine hours of it. Avoid overexertion. Eat good, clean food.

Keep away from houses where there are cases of influenza.

If sick, no matter how slightly, see a physician.

If you have had influenza, stay in bed until your doctor says you can safely get up.

Keep clean. Isolate your patients.

To Nurses:

When in attendance upon patients, wear a mask which will cover both the nose and the mouth. When the mask is once in place, do not handle it.

Change the mask every two hours. Owing to the scarcity of gauze, boil for half hour and rinse, then use the gauze again.

Wash your hands each time you come in contact with the patient. Use bichloride of mercury, 1-1000, or Liquor Cresol compound, 1-1000, for hand disinfection.

Obtain at least nine hours' sleep in each twenty-four hours. Eat plenty of good, clean food. Walk in the fresh air daily.

Sleep with your window open.

Insist that the patient cough, sneeze or expectorate into cloths that may be disinfected or burned.

Boil all dishes. Keep patients warm.

TO AUTOMOBILIST—Help the Cause by Furnishing Free Rides to and From Work to the Limit of Your Cars.

Published Through Courtesy of
THE LANCASTER NEWS
By the Red Cross.

and much of the time Williamson was delirious with fever. He remembers awakening one evening and hearing his doctor ask a nurse, "Is he dead, or is he still with us?" That came as quite a shock to young Williamson.

"But really I should have died," he says. "But there were two things that kept me going. The first was a young French nurse who kept me perked up with double doses of cognac. And the second was my determination to return home and marry my fiance, Myrtle Norman."

Dr. L. W. Fort, now stationed at an army hospital at Ft. McHenry, Maryland, says: "I never saw so many people die. Our commanding general came by one day and said he wanted to talk to the men. 'Well, you better talk to them quick,' I said, 'because 23 died yesterday and the rest might go at any time.' But with all those patients on our hands, we only had two nurses in the entire hospital. One day my best friend was brought to the hospital, and I went to speak with him. But by the time I got there he was already unconscious. The next morning I was passing by the morgue, and the attendant there told me that he had my friend in there—he had died during the night. Then—and I'll never forget this—he told me to look under the next sheets. It was our two nurses.

"But I was scared to death that I would come down with the flu myself. I was surrounded by it all day long, and there were people dying with it right and left. One day I was called over to this big tent they called the death tent. Well, I went inside and that place was stacked with corpses, victims of the flu. Must have been 100 bodies in there. But I decided that if I stayed warm maybe I could avoid it. So I went over to supply and got four wool army blankets. Then I cut the corners off the blankets, thinking that nobody would steal them

Howard K. Williamson (Company E, 323rd Regiment, 81st Infantry Division) with a nurse from the French Red Cross. He was in the hospital for months, suffering from the flu, and said that this nurse saved his life with liberal doses of cognac. He would always remember 1917-18 "as a year of death, nothing but killing or being killed."

Dr. L. W. Fort (far left), now stationed at Ft. McHenry in Maryland, is shown here with army nurses. He lived in fear of coming down with the flu, which was akin to a death sentence in 1918.

The Armistice came hours too late for this poor German lad who died at his post on the morning of November 11, 1918.

if they were cut up that way. So I slept under them at night, and sure enough, nobody ever stole my blankets and I never did get the flu."

THE WAR IN RETROSPECT

To a man, our veterans agree that their experiences in the Great War made them better men. James Caskey says, "Things that had once seemed so unimportant to me as a young man, such as religion, character, and compassion for others, became uppermost in my mind as a result of my experiences in the war."

And Bill Medford nods soberly and says, "I think I matured considerably. After the war I was always comfortable wherever I happened to be, just wherever fate chose to drop me, and with whomever I happened to be with. Whatever arose, I wasn't afraid to tackle it. Like if I was suddenly dropped down in the middle of New York City, that didn't faze me a dern bit either, because I'd been to London and Paris and all those other exotic foreign places. In other words, I just lost my childish reluctance to go places and do things. After you've survived bullets and gas and starvation, there isn't too much left to be afraid of."

And to a man, our veterans approve of America's involvement in the Great War.

W.B. Adams, for example, says of the Kaiser: "If I could of got my hands on him, I wouldn't have shot him, I would've tore out his goozle."

Yet our veterans condemn wars in general. Indeed, Dr. J.C. Harris summed up the feelings of most when he said, "War at any time is bad for all concerned. Still, in the Bicentennial Year of our history, we should all remember that anything worth having is worth striving for. As Abraham Lincoln once said, 'A house divided will surely fall.' That means unless we rally together and give our all to keep America free, we could very well lose our freedom. Certainly this is an excellent time to forget our differences and remember our likenesses. And it's an excellent time to remember all those millions of fine young patriots who gave their all to make our nation what it is."

INDEX